D0713201

COMMUNITY APPROACHES TO CHILD WELFARE

Community Approaches
to Child Welfare
International perspectives

Edited by
LENA DOMINELLI
Professor of Social and Community Development
Department of Social Work Studies
University of Southampton

Ashgate
Aldershot • Burlington USA • Singapore • Sydney

Published by
Ashgate Publishing Limited
Gower House
Croft Road
Aldershot
Hants GU11 3HR
England

Ashgate Publishing Company
131 Main Street
Burlington,
Vermont 05401-5600
USA

Ashgate website:http://www.ashgate.com

Reprinted 2000

British Library Cataloguing in Publication Data
Community approaches to child welfare : internataional
    perspectives. -(C.E.D.R.)
    1. Child welfare
    I. Dominelli, Lena II. University of Southampton. Centre for
    Evaluative & Developmental Research
    362.7

Library of Congress Catalog Card Number: 98-73856

ISBN 1 84014 942 6

Printed and bound in Great Britain by Biddles Limited,
Guildford and King's Lynn.

Contents

List of Contributors

Marilyn Callahan is Professor of Social Work and Co-ordinator of the Child, Family and Community Research Group at the University of Victoria, Canada. She has written extensively about feminist thinking in child welfare and has recently completed research projects on women, pregnancy and substance abuse. Her research approach emphasises the importance of women's experiences in social services and the invisible work women do when receiving a service. She has also worked in feminist organisations designed to re-create services.

Lena Dominelli, Professor of Social and Community Development, is President of the International Association of Schools of Social Work and the Director of the Centre for International Social and Community Development located in the Department of Social Work Studies at the University of Southampton, England where the European Union - Canada Project, *Child Abuse, Protection and Welfare* is housed. She has worked in social services, probation, and community organisations. She has researched and published extensively and has authored 15 books, the most recent of which are: *Anti-Racist Probation Practice* (with others); *Anti-Racist Social Work* (second edition); *Sociology for Social Work*; and *Social Work: Current Themes, Dilemmas and Debates* (with others).

Joan Gilroy retired in June 1998 as Director and Associate Professor at the Maritime School of Social Work at Dalhousie University, Canada to become an Honorary Professor. Her teaching, scholarly, professional and community work is focused on feminism and social work. She did her graduate study in social work, sociology and women's studies at Dalhousie and the University of Toronto. She was a founding member and Chair of the Women's Caucus of the Canadian Association of Schools of Social Work and the International Association of Schools of Social Work.

Greger Helin is an experienced practitioner who works with children and families in Stockholm, Sweden. He specialises in managing projects and practises network therapy. He is the Co-ordinator responsible for the Älvsjö Project, a Swedish neighbourhood located in the capital. Through its activities, it has initiated a number of novel ways of empowering families in the community over a period of years.

Nicoline Isacson is an experienced social worker who co-works with Greger Helin in the Älvsjö Project in Sweden. She is also an experienced networking therapist who has undertaken the co-ordination of several projects in her country over the years. She is keenly committed to empowering parents in their interaction with social work agencies.

Shirley Jackson is a Lecturer in Social Work at the University of Southampton, England. She is a qualified social worker who has practised in a number of fields and settings, particularly in youth justice. Before taking up her current post in 1994, she was the Advice and Policy Worker for the Family Rights Group in London. She has a long-standing interest in user empowerment and has written extensively on the subject, initially in child welfare and latterly on Family Group Conferences in youth justice.

Bill Lee is Associate Professor of Social Work and teaches and does research in community practice and policy at the School of Social Work at McMaster University in Canada. The third edition of his book, *Pragmatics of Community Organisation,* will be published in January 1999.

Mehmoona Moosa-Mitha is an Assistant Professor at the University of Victoria, Canada. She has also worked as a Reviewing Officer for children in the care of Brent Social Services in London, England. She has also held a Fellowship at the London School of Economics and Social Sciences.

Paul Nixon is a Commissioning Officer for Family Group Conferences in Hampshire County Council Social Services Department in England. A qualified social worker, he has worked with children with disabilities in the USA and for several years with Durham and Hampshire County Councils, predominantly in child protection. A member of the initial national pilot group of Family Group Conferences (FGCs), he has practised as a social worker using FGCs and provided training and consultancy in the UK and abroad.

Marilyn Taylor is an experienced social worker and community worker, currently working in southern England. She has worked in both voluntary and statutory settings. She has worked in the Family Group Conference (FGC) environment for several years and is currently a FGC Co-ordinator.

Acknowledgements

In a book like this one which has a number of contributors, each of whom is responsible for their own work, there are bound to be differences of views and emphasis. But rather than being problematic, such diversity should make for more interesting reading.

No book is ever written by a single author or group of authors. Many people contribute to its conceptualisation and transcription. These contributions are often unacknowledged and unrecognised for a number of reasons. Sometimes it is because the authors may not be aware that their store of knowledge and wisdom has been added to by someone else. At other times, the offering is very evident to the writer(s), but hard to attribute to one particular individual. Each of these contributions is a gift and this book is replete with examples of all kinds. To those who have made their mark on our understanding, but whose names may not be known, or who cannot be specifically identified, all of us who have written in these pages express our deepest appreciation for your assistance in our work. It may have been no more than a chance conversation, but nonetheless, its impact may have been the profound one which questioned our taken-for-granted assumptions and facilitated more open thinking on our part. For your challenge was tempered with understanding and patience so that we were enabled to further reflect on our individual views.

Others have contributed overtly and deliberately to our work. This can be said, for example, of the Canadian government and the European Commission who made funds available through their Canada-European Community Programme for Co-operation in Higher Education and Training for us to conduct the project entitled, *Child Abuse, Protection and Neglect*, which made possible the collaboration between Canada, the Netherlands, Sweden and the United Kingdom, which led to this publication. Similarly, our own academic and field institutions have supported our efforts in a variety of ways. We could not have done this work without the active endorsement of all of these organisations. Thank you all for your tolerance and invaluable help.

To our colleagues and friends, we also owe a debt of gratitude. You said kind words when we needed encouragement, gave our work a critical gaze when you challenged our poorly thought out responses to difficult questions and enabled us to produce a better text. To our families and loved ones, we thank you for your love, understanding and forbearance. To all our children, whether or not we are parents, we thank you for making us think more deeply about the world you inhabit and how we adults can assist you in becoming independent beings from birth. The future is yours. We hope to build it with you.

Lena Dominelli
July 1998

To all the world's children, may they be cherished

1 Introducing International Perspectives in Child Welfare

LENA DOMINELLI

Introduction

Ensuring the welfare of children is universally espoused as a concern by adults throughout the world. However, the responses to its realisation are varied and diverse. They also tend to be locality-based with an adherence to particular cultural traditions and legislation which is strictly enforced by those who design any given child welfare system and are deemed to be in charge of it. Caring for children is also considered a 'private' matter of intense interest to the child's birth parents and related kin. The broader community tends to maintain its distance from the family hearth save in exceptional circumstances. The constraints that these particularities impose can mean that social work practice in the child welfare arena can be fairly parochial and the idea that there are *international* perspectives within it which merit consideration can seem strange and uninteresting to those involved in front-line work with children and/or their families.

Yet, there are pressing issues in child welfare which have an international dimension which it is critical for practitioners to address in order to intervene more effectively locally, for example, the global trade in children for the purposes of prostitution and other forms of sexual abuse, child abductions, or transnational adoptions. However, an international framework for intervention in these areas is markedly lacking. The legislation which exists to deal with these matters is usually inadequate. And, it leaves pending the question of how an international perspective in social work which respects cultural traditions and simultaneously enhances the well-being of children can be created and promoted.

The failure of professional practice to engage with the global aspects of social problems has also meant that there is a dearth of materials which examine international perspectives in social work with children and families, particularly from the position of having an international framework which can help make sense of certain developments in a given locale. Though essential for training and practice purposes in a globalising world, developing such a framework is difficult. For it must provide the tools whereby the borders of the nation-state can be transcended while still defending the interests of children in retaining their individual uniqueness and upholding a family's desire that its children retain their group identity with regards to cultural traditions, language and religion.

Working through these concerns involves carefully negotiating a minefield of moral and ethical dilemmas. These may pit practitioners against parents, their children or both, especially if value judgements about behaviours and attitudes are being made. Some of these conflicts may be unavoidable. For example, a social worker who has the responsibility of ensuring the safety of the child may find that he or she has to thwart parental aspirations regarding child-rearing matters if issues of child abuse and neglect are being investigated. There are no straightforward answers to tricky questions such as: 'Who decides which cultural practice might endanger a child's health? On what grounds can the decision be made? How will it be done? When can it be taken? and: Where shall it take place?'

However, given the commonality of many social problems affecting children, we should be able to formulate an international perspective that gives adequate responses to the questions posed. Doing so successfully requires that we acknowledge both similarities and differences in the position of children throughout the world and look towards how we may enforce children's rights so that they can be given greater responsibility in ensuring that their own growth and development proceeds along lines acceptable to them. It also requires that a stronger partnership be established amongst children, parents and those others living in their communities including non-parent adults and professional child welfare workers.

This chapter introduces the key concepts of: childhood as a historically specific phenomenon; inalienable children's rights; community approaches to child welfare; and professional interventions consistent with the concern to promote a child's growth to their full potential.

Childhood: A Socially Constructed Historical Entity

Children represent the future of society and are a precious resource that adults have in their safekeeping. In other words, children are to be held in trust until they reach an age in which they are able to make their own decisions about their affairs. Consequently, the relationship between children and adults should be one in which adults uphold and maintain children's rights. That is, they should treat them as independent or sovereign human beings with rights of their own from birth, that is, as holders of inalienable rights. Sadly, the reality for children in Western societies is that they have been constrained into becoming dependent beings with few autonomous rights as they make the passage from childhood to adulthood.

The nature and period of the transition from childhood to adulthood has varied in length according to historical epoch and custom (Aries, 1962). At the end of the 20th century, the time young people in the West spend in enforced dependency on their parents seems to be expanding. So, for example, young people in Britain who decide to continue studying into tertiary level education may find that government assistance is means-tested on their parents' as well as their own income even though they have long since passed the age of majority, usually taken to be 21. Yet, they can marry without parental consent at 18 or start their own 'family' without this approval with the onset of puberty. Similar conditions prevail in Canada and Sweden.

Financial and proprietorial linkages between children and their parents have an ancient pedigree. Indeed, it was not that long ago that children were considered chattels in whom parental property rights were vested (Fox Harding, 1997). These might have been differentiated according to the gender, age or class of the child. So, for example, primogeniture in aristocratic families gave the oldest male child the right to inherit property and privileged him over his siblings. Though this prerogative has been whittled away in modern times, it continues to be practised within certain segments of the population, particularly its wealthiest elements. An illustration of this is in the British Royal Family, where the oldest son continues to hold the right to inherit the throne.

Childhood exists as a historically developed category which has been ascribed different meanings at different points in time (Aries, 1962). The creation of childhood as a prolonged period of dependency upon biological parents for physical nurturance, financial security and emotional support received a considerable boost during the Victorian era (Aries, 1962). In this variant, children were also considered asexual beings. Moreover, childhood became defined as a time of innocence in which children were in need of adult protection. Yet, this picture of childhood belied the reality for many, particularly working-class and poor children where parents lacked the material wherewithal to provide for them (see Stedman Jones, 1971). So, many Victorian children were compelled to fend for themselves on the mean streets of large, urban conurbations. Material hardship, homelessness, social isolation and boredom with the constancy of the basic struggle to survive, shaped the conditions of the daily lives of children living in such localities then and continue to do so now. Nevertheless, despite considerable evidence which contradicts this rosy picture, the Victorian idyll of a carefree childhood acquired a mythical status which has persisted until the present day.

Children's lot in the community in which they live can be a varied one which ranges from middle-class cacooning in a well-resourced environment to hardship and privation in a poor one. Childhood can be marred through a number of conditions. Crucial amongst these are the absence of adequate financial resources for a child's development and the abuse of children by those responsible for their care. On the economic front, poverty amongst children is higher than amongst adults (Wilkinson, 1994). For example, in the European Union, about a third of children are in poverty compared to about a fifth of adults. The picture is similar in other regions of the globe (UNDP, 1998).

Thus, many children are being deprived of economic stability and the life enhancing opportunities which are associated with it. Poverty stunts their growth and disadvantages them on a number of different dimensions - longevity, nutrition, education, health, income earning potential and housing space. Furthermore, its repercussions follow them throughout their lives. Similar difficulties around low income bedevil the realisation of children's potential in Canada and Sweden (Mishra, 1990). Moreover, their financial difficulties are likely to be exacerbated if children live in a family headed by a lone mother. According to the United Nations Development Programme Report (UNDP, 1998), 8 per cent of children in the rich OECD countries and half of those in single parent families mainly headed by women in Australia, Canada, the United Kingdom and the United States, live below the income poverty line of 50 per cent of median disposal personal income. Thus, dire poverty can be found amongst women and children amidst growing affluence.

Unfortunately, despite the obstacles that severe financial hardship imposes on the growing child, freedom from poverty has not been defined as a basic human right, although the United Nations has encouraged its member states to eradicate child poverty by the year 2000. But, there is no compulsory or enforceable duty of care for children in this regard on either the state or their parents. If the children can subsist from day-to-day and be kept safe from harm, the current position is that there will be no public form of intervention to develop the child's full potential. Yet, the lack of monetary means has prevented large numbers of the world's children from becoming all that they can be (see UNDP, 1998 for the latest global figures on poverty and children world-wide). Instead, they are compelled to scrabble about for a living in the interstices between low-grade technological know-how in the labour market and survival tactics in mean streets.

Moreover, children are denied emotional fulfilment when they are subjected to child abuse and neglect, whether this is of a physical, emotional or sexual nature. The damage that such treatment causes to children can be long-lasting and devastating. Yet, many children endure the violation of their core being on a daily basis. That large numbers of children have been subjected to such disregard of their basic human rights has been hard for adults in their societies to accept. There continues to be an enormous degree of denial and disbelief voiced about the high levels of child sexual abuse that have come to public notice (Campbell, 1988; Gordon, 1985; Bagley and Thurston, 1996). That children are having to live within such precarious circumstances is an indictment of adults' failure to cater responsibly for the needs of the children in their care. In short, a betrayal of trust has occurred.

5

Professional Intervention and the Private Domain of the Nuclear Family

Social workers intervene in such situations to ensure that the welfare of children is maintained. However, social workers, as agents of the state in which they live, are required to operate within a prescribed legal framework and to reinforce the social arrangements which are in force in the child's place of abode. In Western countries, the nuclear family, particularly when it is in crisis or in danger of breaking down, continues to be the basis of their involvement (Hetherington, 1998). The nuclear family has become the yardstick for policy makers (Eichler, 1983; Dominelli, 1991). And, practitioners treat families which deviate from this norm as aberrant.

The nuclear family is taken to consist of one woman, the biological mother and one man, the biological father, married to that woman. Within this arrangement, the woman is responsible for nurturing the children, the man for ensuring the family's economic survival. Yet, this set-up has been a declining family type for some time (Eichler, 1983). Nonetheless, the focus of the social workers' endeavours tends to be upon the mother. The father, though often the perpetrator of many forms of abuse, is usually sidelined.

Only recently, has this state of affairs in social work practice begun to change and the involvement of non-parental others close to the child been legitimated. For example, in England and Wales, the 1989 Children Act gave a child's birth relatives the right to directly approach the courts regarding having residential orders made in their favour, that is, for the child to live with them. Under this legislation, birth parents do not lose their parental rights. In Canada, grandparents are currently seeking to change the law to give them rights to assume care for the child.

Social workers' preoccupation with the nuclear family has diminished the range of interventions which could be practised by limiting the options which they can explore to those that fall within its remit. Consequently, whether human or material, the full extent of the resources which can be accessed by the social worker have been reduced. Thus, a number of people within the extended family who might have had an interest in supporting the child at particular points in his or her life have been excluded from participating in the child's care plans, assisting the child

6

during a period of crisis or facilitating his or her general development. For example, grandparents, are constantly overlooked as a source of support for grandchildren in need. Alternatively, near kin may find caring responsibilities imposed upon them with little discussion and formal support forthcoming to help them carry out their tasks. The legal emphasis on the nuclear family has reinforced the professional view that other family forms are deviant (Eichler, 1984; Dominelli, 1991).

Moreover, within the nuclear family setting, the balance of power between children and parents is heavily weighted towards the latter. Children, as dependent beings have few resources or other bases of power through which to enforce their own views about their life situation and how they would like to see it develop. The advocates of children's rights have sought to address this position. However, much of their efforts have been oriented towards policy and legislative changes at local level. In only a few countries has this preoccupation been extended to encompass the international arena. But these endeavours have brought few additional public resources children's way, although safeguards for children's interests have been initiated in a few places. For example, in Britain, the court can appoint advocates to act in the child's behalf. In Sweden, there is an Ombudsperson that serves to enforce similar concerns. In Canada, welfare falls under provincial jurisdiction, so the arrangements can vary. But British Columbia, for example, introduced a Child, Youth and Family Advocate in 1995 to give 'voice' to the interests of children.

International Dimensions in Child Welfare

The attempt to remedy the lack of formal parity between the rights of children and those of adults has resulted in an international agreement promoted under the aegis of the United Nations (UN). Known as the UN Convention on the Rights of the Child, it has sought to enshrine the child's entitlement to develop to the full, his or her own potential, regardless of which country he or she lives within, or which political system he or she is under. Although the agreement has been ratified by all but two countries since 1989 when it was first promulgated, subsequent monitoring has revealed that even signatory states have been remiss in the observance of its requirements. So, for example, Britain which ratified most parts of the Convention in 1991 was castigated for its failure to meet the necessary

7

conditions when these were checked out in 1995 (Lansdown, 1995). Thus, it seems that although the Convention on the Rights of the Child could provide a framework which could be used as the basis for an international perspective for working with children, it has not lived up to its promise. Nonetheless, social workers could, if they wished, use its provisions to facilitate the recognition of children's rights to a greater extent than they do.

But, because much of social work training is based upon family models operating within the private domain in a given nation-state, social workers experience considerable difficulty in linking up with communities through non-family agents whether at the neighbourhood level or in the international arena. In many ways, they need to re-educate themselves in community-based forms of interventions and acquire community work skills to do the job that is required of them. However, it is not enough to simply focus on obtaining information about the culture of a community. Social workers have to learn how to negotiate with its members in ways that ensure that the interests of the child are best served.

Another part of the problem is that of having rights based on the notion of an individual's entitlement to them. For this individualises the matter and focuses attention on particular families when many others may be suffering similar difficulties in acting as enablers of children's rights. This approach to children's welfare also restricts community involvement in their daily enactment to a considerable extent because the care that nuclear families offer children is held to be a private matter in which neither the community nor the state should become involved. The division between the public and private domains is crucial to maintaining the sanctity of the nuclear family as a domain in which parents reign supreme. And, it reinforces the tendency for policy makers to see family policy as primarily a matter of national jurisdiction.

State intervention, even at the national level, is, therefore, sanctioned only in extreme cases when families fail to provide for their children. The rights of the family, to the extent that they exist, are vested primarily in parents as adults. Thus, I would argue that current legislation affecting children and families in Western countries is largely of a paternalistic nature which presumes that biological families provide the best safeguards for children's well-being and that in most circumstances, they can be left to get on with the task. Privacy in familial situations can act as a major obstacle to investigations that seek to determine whether or not children's right to a secure existence has been violated by the adults responsible for their care. Sadly, the state, acting in *loco parentis* can also replicate similar conditions of unaccountability. The rights of the carers it employs to do what they think is best for children has accounted in part for a number of major scandals pertaining to the abuse of children in residential care (see Haig-Brown, 1988; Levy and Kahan, 1991; Kirkwood, 1992; Pringle, 1992)

Linda MacLeod (1980) argues that violence against women and children in Western society is ignored by neighbours and close others who may be in a position to intervene in family situations and the professional emphasis becomes one of 'stranger danger' because the private-public divide is held to be sacred. This makes the enforcement of reporting requirements difficult for most people who feel they would be interfering in someone else's affairs were they to do so. Even in jurisdictions such as Canada where reporting known cases of child abuse is mandatory and legally punishable if this does not happen, there are many instances in which no one has reported the matter to the child welfare authorities. And yet, rarely has any one been prosecuted for a failure on the part of the community to care for its children.

Hence, under the nuclear family model of intervention, the community from which the child is drawn can also be excluded from becoming involved in sustaining him or her during difficult periods in his or her life by adults' entitlement to privacy. The power adults hold over children within both the private sphere of reproduction encapsulated by acts of parenting and that authorised by the state acting, through its agents as a social parent on behalf of the biological ones, constitutes adultism. Adultism as perpetrated throughout the globe also contributes to the failure of concerned individuals and organisations to mount an effective international position on children's rights.

Community Approaches to Child Welfare

The 'community' to which a child is affiliated can be a locality, religious or culturally based one. Sometimes, these converge into one as in the case of a child of Jewish origins living in Hendon, a Jewish neighbourhood in

9

London, for example. Yet, I would argue that the community, as the space within which the child is embedded, shares a collective responsibility to care for him or her. Thus, all those living in the community in question have a responsibility of caring for all the children living within it. This commitment applies to all adults whether or not they are parents because the bonds of interdependence which exist between them form the bedrock of solidarity across the generations. But a community does not exist outside of the relationships which are established between the individual child and those who represent their community. Representation can be formal or informal and draw on kinship, friendship or *ad hoc* ties.

Consequently, social workers need to understand the nature of the community within which the child lives and develop professional relationships with those who can act on his or her behalf in order to mediate amongst the widest possible groupings for the provision of the supports necessary for a particular child. In addition, to ensure cultural and ethnic representation, a number of social workers should be drawn from all groupings that constitute a particular community. Their roles as representatives of that community is a contingent one that may include assisting in the creation of services appropriate to their specific locale.

Yet, in any given situation, working within the interstices of the community and the family, however these may be defined, is extremely difficult. It may require skills which the social workers do not readily have and therefore necessitate their acquiring additional training. Besides having wisdom and understanding, social workers have to act as negotiators who can mediate between conflicting interests in the complex situations which they encounter. Their ability not to do this effectively can be especially problematic in cases of child sexual abuse. Not only is the social worker often placed in the position of challenging hegemonic ideologies and stereotypes about the protective family and the role of men and masculinity with in it, but the interests of the child may be in direct conflict with those of the parents, especially if one of them happens to be an abusing one.

Recent public enquiries into serious child abuse and neglect indicate that it can be relatively easy for social workers to either over-react or under-react in such situations and intervene inappropriately. Additionally, the child may be further disadvantaged or abused by their interventions (O'Hagan, 1994). Secondary or institutional abuse, as it has been called, can occur in cases where the child has been removed from the protective custody of the parent(s) and placed in either an unknown family setting or a residential institution for it places the burden of handling the disruption which results upon the child. On the other hand, if the parent has been made to leave, the child may struggle with feelings of guilt for they may not have wanted the parent to be removed, only for the abuse to stop.

Yet, children are seldom fully consulted or given the right to decide what steps are necessary to ensure their safety. Nor are they likely to be asked how they might envisage this outcome being achieved. As a result, the child may feel responsible for outcomes over which she or he has had no control. Indeed, the experience of *Childline* in the United Kingdom indicates that children refuse to fully disclose sexual abuse to caring professionals for fear of suffering institutional abuse if they have to appear before the courts to give testimony or if they feel responsible for the initiation of criminal proceedings against one of their parents or close relatives, especially if incarceration is the outcome.

Working in these conditions requires that social workers learn how to share their power in family situations with important others in the community. The ability to do this is essential, for example, in carrying out the injunctions of the Maori approach to working with children and families that is described in chapter six by Shirley Jackson and Paul Nixon. However, it is not easy to achieve such aspirations. Social workers find it difficult to relinquish power when they carry the legal responsibility for ensuring the well-being of the child. Consequently, parents' experience of social workers' power-sharing endeavours can be tokenistic displays of rhetoric in action.

Parents have persistently complained of their lack of influence in child care proceedings. Some of them have formed organisations through which they can link up with others who have had similar experiences to advance their points of view, for example, Family Rights Group, Parents Against Injustice (PAIN). Children, particularly those who have been in care, have also organised to challenge their exclusion from decisions which affect their lives. For example, the Youth in Care Network in Canada and the National Association of Young People in Care and the Black and In Care Group in Britain, have been formed to counter this situation. Fortunately, however, as Marilyn Taylor demonstrates in chapter seven, there are also examples of positive social work intervention in family conflicts. In

11

several of her illustrations, good working partnerships have been established between caring professionals and their clients.

Generally, however, parents, particularly white middle-class ones, are usually left to get on with their work of rearing their children with little external interference by the state, caring professionals or lay persons within the community. Consequently, social workers tend to intervene in family crises that occur largely amongst white working-class (Franklin, 1986) or 'black' families (Barn, 1993)[1]. Though short-sighted as policies endorsing this position are, prevention, these days, is considered a luxury which the state cannot afford to fund. Yet, early intervention could thwart a deterioration in difficult situations between parents and their children.

Working in the community to mobilise community resources in support of children can be an important dimension in promoting preventative approaches to child welfare. Preventative approaches are those which seek to promote the well-being of children in their own surroundings - before a dreadful event occurs. In this way, these attempt to avoid the need for crisis interventions which can be costly, emotionally draining, disruptive of children's growth and development, and psychologically traumatising. However, preventative work in the child welfare arena may require social workers to challenge some of their most cherished social myths. One of these, for example, is the widely-held view that families are the best providers of protective spaces for children. Their questioning of these widely held beliefs may put social workers on a collision course with many 'respectable' members of society and those who uphold traditional family structures or morès including in instances of child sexual abuse (see Bell, 1986).

For even if a social worker is not overtly working towards the abolition of 'the nuclear family', his or her work in the child welfare arena may imply such an agenda. In any case, practitioners may be accused of working towards such an end and find the weight of the judicial system backing their accusers rather than them. This has happened in instances of recovered memory or false memories of child sexual abuse (Pendergrast, 1995). In these, therapists have been blamed for encouraging their adult 'patients' to 'recall' incidents of child sexual abuse which those accused of these assaults persistently declare never happened. The difficulty is that an allegation of childhood sexual abuse that occurred some time ago cannot be easily proven because the evidence to meet the standards of forensic science is no longer available, if it ever were. But, in these cases, the word of the accused - usually a male, is taken more seriously than that of the accuser who is usually female (Cowburn and Dominelli, 1998).

Blaming the bearer of potentially disruptive tidings has also been upheld in the media's handling of social workers' intervention in cases of child sexual abuse. A classic illustration of this response occurred in relation to the child sexual abuse uncovered in Cleveland, England. Here, the feminist social worker and paediatrician who discovered a high incidence of it were subjected to intense media abuse (Nava, 1988). It took a further ten years for their initial findings to be publicly vindicated (Campbell, 1997²). In the meantime, both women had lost their jobs and been compelled by circumstances to move elsewhere to earn their livelihoods.

Yet, if social workers do not challenge some of these dominant stereotypes, they would not be doing their jobs vis-a-vis protecting the interests of the child. As the reactions against them when they do so in relation to male violence against women and children, have demonstrated, practitioners are taking substantial risks. This is because preventative approaches to child sexual abuse have problematised hegemonic masculinity and made it a target of their interventions. As a result, for example, probation work with sex offenders has moved on to include an examination of sex offenders' expectations about themselves as men and their relationships with others who are in positions of dependency with regards to them. Similar insights are being used in work with men who have physically assaulted woman partners in intimate relationships in what have become known as situations of domestic violence (Cavanagh and Cree, 1995; Mullender, 1996).

Following the unearthing of a substantial number of high profile child abuse and neglect cases, child welfare practice in Britain has become protection oriented, that is, it emphasises child protection and crisis intervention at the expense of preventative strategies (Fox Harding, 1997). Similar moves have become evident in British Columbia in Canada, following the Gove Enquiry Report into the death of Matthew Vaudreuil whilst he was in state care. But although individual social workers have been castigated for poor practice in these examples, the community's failure to ensure care in a more general sense passes without remark.

Additionally, child welfare practice is dominated by experts and gives both parents and children a minimal role in the deliberations concerning professional interventions. Expert-led systems have made it difficult for parents to feel that they control the conditions under which they raise their children. Moreover, as Nicoline Isacson and Greger Helin demonstrate in chapter eight, the suspicion that parents may be falling short of the practitioners' anticipated standards of child-rearing does not facilitate parents feeling capable in and responsible for their children's upbringing. Such dynamics are exacerbated when differences across gender, 'race' or other social divisions are involved.

Families that are different from the white middle-class heterosexual norm are deemed deviant and their child-rearing methods are often found wanting. As a result, the children from such families are more likely to be over-represented in the care system (Dominelli, 1988; Barn, 1993). The statistics which underpin this picture belie the larger community's inability to reflect the composition of its population and the domain of the nuclear family yardstick in assessing other patterns of child-rearing.

Moreover, the impact of globalisation with its exaggerated emphasis on managerialism has subjected professional child care practice to increasing scrutiny and monitoring for effectiveness and efficiency (Dominelli and Hoogvelt, 1996). 'Value for money' and bureaucratised forms for evaluating 'client' satisfaction have replaced the exercise of professional judgement carried out on the basis of conducting a considered investigation of the issues causing concern in ways which responds to both the uniqueness of the individual child and the social circumstances he or she occupies because he or she holds membership of a particular social grouping (Dominelli, 1997). Bureaucratising social work intervention with children and families through managerialist control also impedes client involvement in child care decision-making unless it is to complain about an event after the fact. It has been a major factor in members of the public feeling disenfranchised when they do raise concerns about the way a particular parent treats that children with whom they share homes.

Intervening in child welfare situations requires giving attention to complex situations involving a wide range of skills, not all of which may be held by the individual practitioner. Linking up with other professionals, particularly those addressing health issues, schooling, psychological development and housing, call for interdisciplinary team working. A corps of such people may be hard to establish in practice because inter-professional rivalries can impede their working together effectively. Problems in communication across the professional divides, differences in values and opinions about the 'correct' way to proceed can inhibit collaboration between different professional groupings. Improving interagency communication and the delivery of services to children in care has been commented upon by a series of child care reports, including the Utting Report (Utting, 1991) in the UK because information provided by individuals reporting to one agency are not always passed on to the others.

However, interdisciplinary team working, when it is successfully implemented can be empowering of both the professionals and the parents involved. Nicoline Isacson and Greger Helin discuss a successful interdisciplinary partnership which draws on the broader community in a Swedish district in chapter eight. In it, they demonstrate how social workers must intervene at a range of levels - the macro, meso and micro, for professionals who work together to effectively offer support to families who have reached the bottom line in coping with the difficulties they have encountered. Moreover, their interventions are aimed at preventing children coming into care. Their preferences are to have children flourish in their own communities with their families.

Supporting families is an important if under-utilised aspect of a local authorities' consideration of community approaches to child welfare. However, community approaches can also be exploited by public and private commercial agencies seeking to offload their responsibilities to provide services to children and families in need by asking their (extended) families to accept the duty of caring for their relatives in unpropitious circumstances. This often means that women get called upon to provide free labour time and other unpaid forms of support. Yet, in many communities, these same women may already be overburdened with unpaid work as they seek to overcome the gap between the resources they and their families need, and those that are actually available to them. Such demands on women may also mean that the health and well-being of the women themselves can be damaged, thereby feeding a cycle of decline which leaves them and their families short-changed. This can include the lack of food, leisure time or facilities aimed at meeting the needs of women as women in their own right instead of in their roles as mothers and wives.

Children's Rights

Children's rights is an ambiguous and contested notion. Whilst those advocating children's rights are child-centred, the two concepts - child-centredness and children's rights are not contiguous. The balance of power between children and parents can differ substantially between these two positions. Those promoting the rights of the child tend to give a greater weighting to children's right to act as autonomous beings making decisions about their own welfare and according them a similar legal status to that of the adult. A child-centred approach can include paternalistic concerns being displayed with regards to advancing children's development whilst decision-making powers lie firmly in the laps of the parent(s). Regardless of the perspective taken regarding the appropriate form of care for children, those endorsing children's rights usually conceptualise them in ways which pit the rights of the child against those of the parents and those of the parents against those of the state (see Fox Harding, 1997).

It has to be acknowledged that parents do gain from having children and holding power over them, for example, the status which accrues to women as mothers. However, these are not unalloyed pleasures. The interests of women as women can be in conflict with those of children as children. But these do not have to be pitted against each other in binary opposition (Dominelli and McLeod, 1989). Drawing a polarised division between the interests of parents and children or between parents and the state is unhelpful in an arena fraught with complexities, ethical dilemmas of various kinds and the existence of interdependent relationships amongst these parties.

These conflicts can be transcended by considering these as interdependent relationships and as caring work which although it is delivered privately in most situations resides in the public domain as work for which adults are held accountable. The partitioning of people's lives into public and private domains in which the later is sacrosanct, particularly within the confines of the family, provides the framework within which parents are given extensive powers over children for which they are rarely held externally accountable. The exceptions to this situation are usually cases of suspected abuse, when state agents are legally entitled to intervene to protect the interests of the child(ren) (MacLeod, 1980). But accountability in this regard is also fragmented. The privatising of child welfare in this way is highly problematic. It is likely to become more so as the state cedes its responsibilities to private for-profit providers.

Reciprocated Social Parenting

For these reasons, I prefer to consider children's rights within the framework of interdependent relationships which involve children, their parents, other adults in the community and the nation-state in which they live. In this context, children's rights can be considered as neither completely autonomous nor completely dependent on others. Additionally, conceptualising children's rights in these terms allows for children to have rights within the context of reciprocity and mutuality between them and those adults who care for them. These may not be their biological parents but they are people who are answerable for their care of them, that is, those whom I consider as undertaking social parenting. Taken in this light, children's rights provide a limitation on parental and adult powers from the standpoint of children's interests as they see them. And, it enables a community to engage in responsible social parenting which meets the conditions of reciprocity.

I would argue that if assisted, children have the capacity to make decisions in their own affairs from a fairly early age. But adults often deny them the opportunity to do so because it suits them for a variety of reasons including the practicalities of life. These may prompt adults into short-changing children, even in non-contentious areas. Their pre-occupations in this regard do not have to be of malevolent intent, but they do indicate the extent to which the balance of power lies with adults unless there is a deliberate attempt to shift it in children's direction.

Children can express their likes and dislikes early on in childhood (Eckelaar, 1992). Adults can facilitate the child's expression of their feelings and views, but often do not, for pressure of time or similar reasons. To demonstrate my point, I take the straight forward example of a child getting dressed. When it comes to choosing what clothes to wear on a particular day, a parent who is stressed out by work commitments and in a hurry will just give a young child a set to put on rather than use the occasion as a chance to help the child decide what clothes he or she wants to wear and how these can be made appropriate to the weather conditions and social situation.

However, for adults to respond in the manner suggested above, they need to have: time to spend with the child(ren); their efforts valued by other adults; and, their parenting activities actively supported as a community endeavour rather than being seen as simply a private choice which individuals take when they 'decide' to have children. Its realisation also requires putting money, emotional support and physical resources behind the carers whether or not they are the child's birth parents or his or her social parents.

Moreover, I would maintain that if the adults responsible for the care of children, whether they are their own or not, take the time to see their interaction with children as a learning opportunity in which their task is to assist children take decisions about their own affairs as they grow to maturity, children's rights could be taken out of the dichotomous context which places them in binary opposition to those of adults. It also means that adults, particularly parents, do not have to automatically be considered as having malicious intentions towards children. Moreover, the application of standards of child care which serve the children's needs do have to be conceptualised as matters which reside in the public domain where they can be articulated and debated in ways that involve children, adults whether or not they are parents and child welfare professionals. Once debated and agreed, these become the standards to which parents, whether biological or social, are held accountable by children and other adults. The simultaneous monitoring of the application of these norms is, therefore, desirable.

Social Parenting

In short, I am advocating the view that parenting has to be seen as a social activity - a matter of social parenting or an act which requires both a collective community responsibility once a child is born and a publicly accountable private responsibility on the part of the parents or adults doing the caring of them. Conceptualising children's rights as reciprocated rights breaks the binary opposition between those of children and adults advocated in the construction of children's rights found in the writings of Franklin (1986) or Freeman (1992).

I use the concept of social parenting to describe parenting situations undertaken by people other than the biological parents of children. This includes members of that child's extended kinship system, friends and neighbours and the state authorising non-related adults to provide parental care for children. The importance of social parenting is that it places parenting in the public rather than the private domain, although it acknowledges that much of the day-to-day work of parenting will take place in the private realm. But public accountability to the child him or herself, other children and adults living in their community and caring professionals becomes the means whereby parenting in the private domain is monitored and can become a matter of concern to others. As a result, those undertaking parenting duties, carrying out parental responsibilities and getting the joy which comes from relating to children, would expect to have to justify their treatment of children if called upon to do so by the children themselves, other adults or child care professionals.

Of course, an investigation has to be launched to establish the adequacy of the standards of care provided in any particular case when it is questioned or even as a matter of regular reporting. But those conducting such an enquiry or monitoring of parental efforts could report to a formally constituted panel made up of children, adults including parents and non-parents, and child care professionals. The procedures governing such an examination would have to be public and accessible. But, an invocation of them should not be taken to imply either guilt or innocence on the part of those doing the parenting. This should be a matter to be determined. Moreover, the fact of undergoing a questioning of their capacities as parents should not carry any stigma.

Such invocations may seem idealistic. But adults do need to rethink their treatment of young people in a planet in which many of the world's children: go to bed hungry every night when the technological means for feeding each of them is available; are uneducated, particularly if they are girls, when survival in modern society requires schooling; and have no homes to go to because shelters for them have not been provided by either their adult carers or communities (UNDP, 1998). Additionally, adults need to call a halt to the exploitation of children across national frontiers for the purposes of adult pleasure. Intergenerational solidarity needs to be built up in those countries which lack it. This requires a recognition of the interdependence of generations and how this varies across the life-cycle. Today's children whom adults care for are those who will respond to the call to care for them in their turn during old age. This book makes a small contribution towards raising the issue of intergenerational reciprocity as expressed through adults treatment of children and the search for ways forward in the creation of a world fit for all children.

Structure of the Book

This book considers the dilemmas and issues contained within community approaches to child welfare and the solutions to practical problems as practitioners and researchers have addressed them in the field by looking at the specific experiences of those at the receiving end of social work interventions in Canada, England and Sweden. Though comparisons may be made, these examples do not provide a comparative study for it is notoriously difficult to find a way of examining these issues across national divides in the absence of an analytical framework capable of meeting the demands required for doing so (Hetherington, 1998). But it does seek to consider how international perspectives can assist in the creation of more child-centred approaches to child welfare.

Thus, the contributions contained within these covers explore community-based initiatives to child welfare which have sought to be child-centred. Moreover, the experiences considered by the academics and practitioners located in Canada, England and Sweden, have led them to call for a redressing of the balance between the rights of the parents, children and public authorities. However, even in pursuing this agenda, the outcome of professional practice can be conventional - that of keeping the child embedded in the community networks in which he or she is located as a result of parental affiliations.

This book is structured as follows. Chapter one by Lena Dominelli provides an introduction to the issues that are encountered in attempting to develop a child-centred perspective that draws on work with children and their families in different countries. In chapter two, Joan Gilroy describes the outcomes of a research project based in Halifax, Canada. In this study, she and her colleagues have obtained the views of practitioners and practice teachers working in the field of child welfare as to the difficulties they encounter when they respond to tighter budgetary restraints whilst at the same time attempting to provide more ethnically sensitive and appropriate services to their users.

Community responses to child welfare become a crucial way of tackling these pressures, especially in the First Nations community of the Mi'kmaqs. The struggles of women to have their voices heard by child welfare professionals in Canada forms the basis of the research considered in chapter three by Marilyn Callahan. Advocating on their behalf, she highlights the strengths that mothers have in negotiating their encounters with welfare professionals and calls for the development of new forms of citizenship which accord these women dignity and recognition.

In chapter four, Bill Lee draws lessons from developments in the Toronto-based Children's Aid Society's efforts to promote community approaches to child welfare in an urban environment. He underlines the impact that macro level forces have in defining the conditions under which ordinary people conduct their business. Whilst their strengths are acknowledged, he argues that structural change has a greater influence on their situations than individual motivation. Thus, organised collective actions needs to exist alongside personal initiatives.

Mehmoona Moosa-Mitha discusses the impact of the 1989 Children Act on children's welfare in the United Kingdom and on the partnership it espoused regarding the work professionals undertook with parents in chapter five. Her research reveals the multiplicity of unmet needs that are endured by young people in care and concludes that the principles of partnership and the formation of new power relations between children, parents and the state are little more than fine words. The community voice is either absent or indifferent enough to condone poor services for children who require the best of care that society can provide. Yet, there is little public outcry against such treatment of a group of children which society has dismissed from its remit of active concerns.

There is more scope for optimism in the contribution that follows hers - the British experience of Family Group Conferences (FGCs). FGCs stem from an idea emanating from New Zealand and is examined in chapter six by Shirley Jackson and Paul Nixon. In it, they raise questions about the extent to which social workers are willing to cede power to children and their families. They are committed to FGCs as a partnership which carries the potential of redressing the balance of power between parents and the state almost in spite of professional reluctance to accede to power sharing.

The theme is continued in chapter seven where Marilyn Taylor describes the experiences of FGCs and the dilemmas posed by them as encountered by a Family Group Conference Co-ordinator. She emphasises the importance of good working relations amongst all the professionals who intervene in any given family situation as well as highlighting the need for practitioners to share power with the parents. She also draws attention to the significance of the workers' interaction with young people in care for the validation of their survival and social skills.

In chapter eight, Nicoline Isacson and Greger Helin recount their efforts in using community-based approaches to empower families in a particular district in Stockholm, Sweden. Their innovations comprise a vertically and horizontally integrated response to supporting families in their own terms while succeeding in getting the local politicians on their side. As a result of their endeavours, parental authority is re-asserted in the parent-child relationship. Moreover, they have found ways of keeping inter-professional groupings going despite a series of changes in their working conditions.

The concluding chapter by Lena Dominelli argues for community-based approaches as a way forward in ensuring that children are considered as people with rights which adults should respect and promote. Embedding them in community networks which do not exploit either their families' resources or their mothers' unpaid labour seems a promising way of promoting the empowerment of children and their parents. However, this has to take place in the context of a supportive environment guaranteed by the state as the guardian of the rights of all its citizens. She concludes by arguing that each adult is responsible for advancing the well-being of all the children in his or her community. Ensuring the realisation of this approach becomes a task for social workers to promote as a preventative strategy which encourages intergenerational solidarity as reciprocated caring for the future at both national and international levels.

Notes

1   I use the term 'black' families in its British usage to describe families who are subjected to racist social relations regardless of their skin-colour. I do not mean to imply that these families form a homogeneous group nor that the problems they encounter in their daily lives do not have their own specific

characteristics. In Britain, 'black' is utilised to mean someone of African or Asian origins.

2   The child abuse scandal in Cleveland, England in 1987 received wide press coverage. In this, the social worker and paediatrician were accused of creating the crisis by falsely accusing men of abusing their children. Although an official enquiry was conducted on the matter, it was not until Channel 4 released a documentary programme on the subject in 1997 that the truth about these allegations finally emerged. Sadly, the majority of children taken into care in 1987 had been sexually abused.

References

Aries, P. (1962), *Centuries of Childhood*, Penguin, Harmondsworth.

Bagley, C. and Thurston, E. (1996), *Understanding and Preventing Child Sexual Abuse: Critical Summaries of 500 Key Studies*, Arena, Aldershot.

Barn, R. (1993), *Black Children in Care*, Batsford, London.

Bell, S. (1987), *When Salem Came to the Boro'*, Penguin, Harmondsworth.

Campbell, B. (1997), *Official Secrets*, Penguin, Harmondsworth, Original published in 1988.

Cavanagh, K. and Cree, V. (1995), *Working with Men from a Feminist Perspective*, Routledge, London.

Cowburn, M. and Dominelli, L. (1998), 'Beyond Litigation: The False Memory Syndrome', *British Journal of Social Work*, vol. 28, no. 4, August, pp. 526-540.

Dominelli, L. (1988), *Anti-Racist Social Work*, BASW-Macmillan, London. Second edition published in 1997.

Dominelli, L. (1991), *Women Across Continents: Feminist Comparative Social Policy*, Harvester/Wheatsheaf, London.

Dominelli, L. (1997), *Sociology for Social Work*, Macmillan, London.

Dominelli, L. and Hoogvelt, (1996), 'Globalisation and the Technocratisation of Social Work', *Critical Social Policy*, vol. 16, no. 2, May, pp. 45-62.

Dominelli, L. and McLeod, E. (1989), *Feminist Social Work*, Macmillan, London.

Eckelaar, J. (1992), 'The Importance of Thinking that Children have Rights', in P. Alston, S. Parker, and J. Seymour (eds), *Children, Rights and the Law*, Clarendon Press, Oxford.

Eichler, M. (1983), *Families in Canada Today*, Gage, Toronto.

Fox Harding, L. (1997), *Perspectives in Child Care Policy*, Longman, London. First published in 1991.

Franklin, B. (ed) (1986), *The Rights of Children*, Blackwell, Oxford.

Freeman, M.D.A. (1992), 'Taking Children's Rights more Seriously', *International Journal of Law and the Family*, vol. 6, pp. 52-71.

Gordon, L. (1985), 'Child Abuse, Gender and the Myth of Family Independence: A Historical Critique', *Child Welfare*, vol. 64, no. 3, pp 213-34.

Hetherington, R (1998), 'Issues in European Child Protection Research', *European Journal of Social Work*, vol. 1, no. 1, pp. 71-82.

Lansdown, G. (1995), 'Children's Rights and Wrongs', *Poverty*, vol. 90, no. 2.

Levy, A. and Kahan, B. (1991), *The Pindown Experience and the Protection of Children*, Staffordshire County Council, Stafford.

MacLeod, L. (1980), *Wife Battering in Canada*, Canadian Advisory Council on the Status of Women, Ottawa.

Mishra, R. (1990), *The Welfare State in Capitalist Society: Policies of Retrenchment and Maintenance in Europe, North America and Australia*, University of Toronto Press, Toronto.

Mullender, A (1998) *Rethinking Domestic Violence: The Social Work and Probation Response*, Routledge, London.

Nava, M. (1988), 'Cleveland and the Press: Outrage and Anxiety in the Reporting of Child Sexual Abuse', *Feminist Review*, no. 28, Spring, pp. 103-121.

O'Hagan, K. (ed) (1996), *Competence in Social Work: A Practical Guide for Professionals*, Jessica Kingsley, London.

Pendergrast, M. (1997), *First of All, Do No Harm*, Skeptic, Denver.

Stedman Jones, G. (1971), *Outcast London*, Clarendon Press, Oxford.

United Nations Development Programme (UNDP) (1998), *Human Development Report, 1998*, United Nations, New York.

Utting, W. (1991), *Children in the Public Care System*, HMSO, London.

2 Critical Issues in Child Welfare: Perspectives from the Field

JOAN GILROY

The Maritime School of Social Work (MSSW) at Dalhousie University in Halifax, Nova Scotia is working with other schools of social work in Canada and Europe on an international project entitled, *Child Abuse, Protection and Welfare*, which is funded by the European Community - Canada Programme for Co-operation in Higher Education and Training[1]. Amongst other activities, this three-year project involves the exchange of social work students who will do their final field placements in child welfare under the auspices of the participating Canadian and European universities. The goals of the project are to compare child welfare policies, services and social work practices in the participating countries, develop curricula which consider child protection and child welfare in an international context, and make recommendations for improving practice in this area.

As part of this project, the team from the Maritime School of Social Work met with staff in the field of child welfare in Nova Scotia[2]. The purposes of these meetings were to inform staff about the Project and solicit their support for its overall goals, to plan exchange-student placements, and to discuss critical issues in the field. In order to develop these curricula, the team from Dalhousie thought it important to refresh and build on their understanding of current issues in child welfare work and to involve child welfare personnel in the process. The focus of this chapter is on the preliminary findings from faculty interviews with field staff.

Child Welfare in Canada and Nova Scotia

In Canada, child welfare is a provincial jurisdiction, as are health, education, and other social services, but the federal government plays a very important role because it provides significant funding. Until it was replaced, the federal Canada Assistance Plan (CAP), enacted in 1966, was the primary social welfare policy, enabling the sharing of costs with the provinces for income assistance (welfare) and social programmes, including child welfare services such as child protection, foster homes, adoption and residential care. The alleviation of poverty was an explicit goal of the CAP programme, which made available provisions for families in need as defined by income. CAP also required that cost-shared services be regulated and administered by government agencies or non-profit organisations.

A major review of Canada's social security programmes took place in the early-1990s at a time when the federal and most provincial governments had large budget deficits, when there was an economic recession with increasing unemployment, which added to the costs of unemployment insurance and welfare programmes, and decreased revenue from taxes. In 1995, the federal government responded to increasing deficits by drastically reducing spending on health, education and social welfare programmes and announcing that a new programme called the Canadian Health and Social Transfer (CHST) would replace both CAP and the funding arrangements that had been established for sharing the costs of health and post-secondary education with provincial governments. Cuts in federal spending and the implementation of block funding under CHST had a devastating effect on the budgets of provincial and territorial governments and on Canada's social programmes. The goals of improving health care, education and social services were replaced by those of deficit reduction by federal, provincial and territorial governments.

With the substitution of block funding under the CHST for federal-provincial sharing of the costs of social services under CAP, social welfare programmes were placed in competition with health and education for reduced amounts of federal money[3]. Cuts in federal spending extended beyond welfare to include unemployment insurance, social housing, and day care, which had particularly negative effects on poor families who are the main users of child welfare services. At a time when caseloads and

26

child poverty are both increasing, child welfare services face even more severe budgetary constraints[4]. Nova Scotia and all of Atlantic Canada have also suffered from the collapse of the traditional fishing industry, rising unemployment, job insecurity, low wages, and changes in unemployment insurance.

Child welfare services are funded through the federal government, but operate under provincial child welfare legislation and regulations. Thus, each province has its own legislation and regulations, policies, and ways of delivering services. In Nova Scotia, the Department of Community Services is responsible for providing or overseeing the provision of child welfare and residential services[5]. These services are delivered throughout the province by district offices of the Department or through privately operated children's aid societies or family and children's service agencies[6]. In addition, the Mi'kmaq Family and Children's Services (MFCS) provides child welfare services for Mi'kmaq families living on provincial reserves - tracts of land especially designated for First Nations people in treaties.

The history of the colonisation has resulted in specific problems being created for the aboriginal peoples of Canada who are now generically referred to as First Nations. In Nova Scotia, the Mi'kmaq Nation are one of the groupings which have recently begun to re-assert their traditional rights to self-determination. Child welfare considerations constitute part of this process. The Mi'kmaq Family and Children's Services of Nova Scotia (MFCS) was formed in 1985 through a tripartite agreement among Canada through the federal Department of Indian and Northern Affairs, the province of Nova Scotia through the Department of Community Services, and the Mi'kmaq Nation through the Chiefs of the thirteen Bands in Nova Scotia. The MFCS's purpose is to provide child welfare and family services to Mi'kmaq women, men and children residing in reserves. Of the 16,000 registered Mi'kmaq in Canada, around 6,000 live on thirteen reserves in Nova Scotia. The MFCS is managed by a Board of Directors who are the Chiefs of the thirteen Bands. The Grand Chief is an honorary member and a representative of the Nova Scotia Native Women's Association.

The majority of residential services for children and adolescents in the province of Nova Scotia are operated by private non-profit boards under policies and standards established by the Department of Community Services. Designated child welfare staff in provincial government offices

27

and children's services agencies throughout the province are mandated under the Children and Family Services Act (CFSA) to investigate all reports of child abuse and neglect[7].

Findings from Meetings with Child Welfare Staff

We began our conversations with child welfare staff by inviting administrators of child welfare agencies and offices in metropolitan Halifax and the Mi'kmaq Family and Children's Services and one or two members of their supervisory and front-line staff, to attend a meeting with the project faculty. Although we initially had planned to hold only one meeting, we were not able to schedule a single time suitable for staff from all the offices and agencies in the area. An advantage to accommodating this need meant that holding more than one meeting with smaller numbers of staff allowed us more opportunity to gather information, give people time to talk, and explore the views and experiences of individual staff members and agencies. In total, we met with eleven staff members, six from provincial government child welfare offices, two from the Halifax Children's Aid Society (CAS) and three from the MFCS[8]. We also interviewed two graduate students who had considerable experience in child protection.

Prior to the meetings held with child welfare staff, we provided brief descriptions about this international child welfare project in newsletters[9], sent preliminary information to social work students and child welfare staff, and briefed the provincial Director of Child Welfare and senior personnel on this project. This preliminary information generated considerable interest among personnel in the field and inquiries from students about doing exchange field placements through the Project.

While conducting the meetings and interviews, as mentioned above, we wanted to inform, solicit support, and focus on critical issues from the perspectives of those working in the field. The information we gathered provided snapshots which will be added to and revised through further interviews and meetings with staff from other areas of Nova Scotia and with undergraduate and graduate students who already have experience in child welfare and/or are interested in doing field placements and getting jobs in child welfare. We see our role in this Project as being the creation of a participatory educational and research framework within which to build social work theory and practice in child welfare.

In the meetings and interviews, we asked three main questions:

1. What are the most critical issues facing you in child protection and child welfare?
2. How have financial restraints affected your work in providing child welfare services?
3. What would be most useful to you and your agency in your efforts to improve the quality of child welfare services?

The interviewees replies to our queries are presented below.

1.   What are the Most Critical Issues Facing You in Child Protection and Child Welfare?

Insufficient resources.   The inadequacy of resourcing was the response given by everyone, whether in front line, supervisory, or administrative positions. Social workers and agencies in child welfare have the authority under the provincial legislation, the Children and Family Services Act, and they are required by law and expected by the public to provide child welfare services, especially to protect children from neglect and abuse, but they do not have sufficient resources to do this work. They do not have the money to employ the number of qualified staff needed to ensure that child welfare standards are met and to ensure appropriate placements of good quality for children in care[10]. The foster home programme is in difficulty, with fewer homes than children needing to be accommodated in foster care, and with fewer foster homes that can accept siblings, or children and teens with acting-out behaviours. There is also a shortage of group homes and of treatment facilities.   Children have to be sent out of the province for intensive residential mental health treatment. But, the scarcity and cost of such treatment programmes have meant that only a few children qualify.

Within the agencies in the metropolitan area of Halifax, scarce resources are allocated to the core mandate, that is, to child abuse and protection referrals, with little left for prevention and the alleviation of less serious problems such as common types of parent-teen conflicts. Measuring preventive work is also problematic. To date, there is almost no documentation or research to substantiate the claim that social work counselling or services of another kind now will prevent expensive problems later - expensive both in human terms and for the system.

Scarce resources are also inadequate to meet the increasing complexity of the personal and family situations coming to the attention of child welfare agencies. Poverty, unemployment, job insecurity, drug abuse by parents, and other health problems, are creating enormous stress for families, with the result that personal problems are more complicated and serious and are showing up at a younger age. As one child welfare worker we interviewed put it:

> Younger and more troubled children are coming into care, and they are not getting the care they need and deserve and that we are mandated to provide.

Social workers are in a continually contradictory position, knowing that they have to provide protective services by law, that they do not have the time and resources to do so, and that they and their agencies are liable if a child dies or is abused or severely neglected. They worry about what will happen to the children if their agencies do not arrive at the best decision after assessments of risk, what will happen if mistakes are made, and whether their best judgement can prevent abuse that may result in injury or even death. According to the staff interviewed, child welfare workers are doing their best to meet the requirements that they assess the family situation, determine risk, and act in the best interests of the child without the necessary time, money, or range of resources. But, they are working at enormous costs to their own health and the integrity and effectiveness of the jobs they do.

This situation places child welfare workers in an ongoing ethical dilemma, given their primary obligation under codes of ethics to act in the best interests of the client and their duty to inform clients of any reasons why they cannot provide services[11].

The changing practice of the social worker. Not only is there not enough funding for sufficient numbers of qualified staff and for resources, but how resources are allocated also shapes the help the workers are able to provide to clients. The *practice* of social workers in child welfare, or the *role* as it is often called, is being changed by the inadequacy and structure of funding, and persons and forces beyond the control of social workers, their professional associations and unions. In the words of one supervisor, 'scarce resources and the structure of funding are driving the practice'.

Practice is being shaped by the lack of sufficient staff. This affects caseload size, what can be done in each situation, even how often social workers can visit and talk with family members about their problems. The Child Welfare League and provincial government standards for child protection are given as twenty cases per worker, and these are to be a mixture of low, medium, and high risk cases. Today, social workers in the metropolitan Halifax region of Nova Scotia are carrying twenty-five to thirty-five cases, and these are mainly determined to be high risk.

Agencies are at times forced to go to court to get particular services paid for, which brings in another complex set of problems, not the least of which is how legal processes influence the relations and the analysis of problems between the social worker and client, most often the mother of the children.

The example was given of a lone woman parent caring for her son, a boy who had neurological problems and a hearing impairment which had remained undiagnosed for a time and had led to speech problems, all of which affected his learning and school performance. Since the only way for the child welfare agency to access services was via the court, the social worker explained to the mother (who had herself been a ward of the court) that she had to begin legal proceedings in order to obtain funds for hearing aids, a speech pathologist, and other required services. This resulted in the mother receiving a social worker contracted through a private agency to help her with parenting, a psychologist to do an assessment on her son, a speech therapist, a legal aid lawyer, and other professional persons to help her and the child. Perhaps as a consequence of all this scrutiny, the woman's parenting was questioned and the notion of apprehending, or of taking the child into care, was considered. Fortunately, that did not happen, but one can see how the ways agencies have to access monies to cover the costs of services can shape the thinking about clients, move options towards taking children into care and shift relations between social workers and clients away from co-operative problem solving and towards investigation and blame.

Lawyers and legal processes were most frequently cited as being influential in the changing and diminished role of the social worker in child welfare. Lawyers are now employed to take cases to court, speak on behalf of the agency, and call social workers as witnesses. Parents are often represented by their own legal-aid lawyers, who request 'independent, objective assessments' as is their right, usually granted and given to psychologists to do. In decisions about taking a child into custody, courts may consider the parental assessments done by a psychologist on contract more unbiased than that of the social worker who apprehended the child. Hearings are scheduled to allow time for new assessments, meaning that the child may be left in a foster home or in care for a considerable time before judgement is made, and then may be returned home. Although the Children and Family Services Act has time limits, children may become considerably dislocated by moving from home to foster home and home again.

The social worker is the person visiting the family, the one with the most knowledge of the people and the problems, but it is other professionals, most often psychologists, whose knowledge is taken as more reliable for the purposes of making decisions in matters of care and custody. Social workers in child welfare experience a loss of recognition of their expertise in their own field, and diminished autonomy and control over their own work. Lawyers, in the view of social workers, can have their own ideas about case management and these can be dominant. Legal processes can be somewhat intimidating for social workers, especially if they are new to the field and inexperienced in working with family courts.

The social worker has increasingly become more of a case manager and broker of services, especially when a court adjourns after requesting an assessment by a psychologist, or when services such as homemakers, and personal or budget counselling need to be organised. Social workers spend more of their time calling together and co-ordinating whatever supports are needed and available, and listening to and reporting on what others are doing and finding. One result can be that a family is overwhelmed by help. In one case cited, thirteen professionals or resource people became involved with a family. The social worker spends more time obtaining resources and co-ordinating services, has less frequent contact with families, yet still retains responsibility for the outcome. Staff interviewed talked about having to do their jobs at 'arm's length,' relying on other professionals to provide information and services. Social workers say they have not been trained to be case managers or brokers of services as their primary role. They wonder how one can become an effective case manager in these circumstances and whether this is the role that ought to be primary.

Child welfare workers do not hearken back to the 'good old days' when social workers presented their own cases in court. They support the increased emphasis on legal and human rights and they recognise the role of the legal profession and legal processes in complicated and sensitive family situations. The resulting practice is, however, more complex and more difficult to carry out according to the knowledge, values, and experiences of social workers in the field and is more likely to be shaped by larger social forces and more powerful professions.

The increasing privatisation of services is also influencing practice in child welfare. As mentioned earlier, government funding is available under the Act for court-ordered services, such as psychological assessments and counselling which are usually referred to psychologists and social workers in private practice. Under the provisions of the legislation, money is also available for family support services. Child welfare workers wonder who benefits from contracting formerly public services to private practitioners, and if the same amount of money would not be better spent in hiring additional social workers and support staff. Social workers feel that their knowledge, skills and daily work are being downgraded, resulting in a loss of self-esteem, self-confidence, and ability to do the job.

Documentation requirements have increased under the new child welfare legislation and regulations, and heightened awareness of issues of liability in cases of child neglect and abuse. Standards and protection manuals are useful, but these and the results of various inquiries into cases have imposed on social workers heavy requirements for documentation. A great deal of time is consumed by preparing information for computer records and by paperwork - time which could be better spent with clients. Standards do not increase resources to do the job, but social work performance is increasingly evaluated by the documentation, by paper. As one worker said:

social workers could give the appearance of doing good work without actually spending much time talking with clients, problem-solving, and so on.

Working conditions. High caseloads, insufficient resources, and the devaluation of their work have become the daily conditions of doing child protection. These lead to stress and loss of confidence among workers who fear they will be unable to provide the services necessary to protect children and assist parents.

Personal safety issues. Personal safety issues are also not being adequately addressed. Child welfare and other social agencies may have security systems which often include barriers between people who come into the agency and the staff. However, social workers' place of employment is not only in the office; they also visit people in their homes. The majority of child welfare workers are women who make home visits alone and have gone into situations of violence, known and unknown, that are sometimes influenced by drinking and drugs. Child welfare staff have been attacked. The police consider domestic disputes as among their most difficult and dangerous calls. However, social workers often enter these sorts of situations with little back up or support.

Individuals are advised to carry mace, to take self-defence courses, and to take police on home visits which they fear will be dangerous. One example was given of a family court judge ordering the home visits of children to be supervised by the police. Social workers do not want to go into their clients homes armed with mace. They also find it difficult to convince anyone that police protection is needed unless there have been previous incidents of violence and they know that police presence inevitably changes the nature of interactions with families.

Although courses on non-violent crisis intervention are offered to social workers, foster parents, and other caregivers, and may be part of core training, safety measures are left for individuals and individual offices to address. In Nova Scotia, occupational health and safety legislation has been proclaimed, but there are few resources to implement the province's Occupational Health and Safety Act.

Liability. There is increasing concern, based on actual case examples, that individual social workers will be held liable for deaths that result from parental neglect or abuse. A social worker in a Toronto Children's Aid Society was recently charged alongside the mother with criminal negligence in the death of a child (*Toronto Star*, 9 August 1997). Social workers recognise the need for accountability, but they fear that they may become scapegoats in tragic deaths of children, that courts and the public will hold them responsible without knowing the case, while the insufficiency of funding for child welfare and other basic services needed by families, and the difficult conditions under which child welfare workers do their jobs, will be ignored. It is too easy, they fear, to blame individuals for the deeply entrenched, systemic problems of poverty, unemployment, addiction, violence, sexism, and racism.

Training issues. Social workers do not feel sufficiently prepared to provide child protection. In Nova Scotia, they are often assigned a caseload as soon as they begin their job. They have supervision and are required to do a two-week core training in child welfare and child protection within the first six months of employment. In other jurisdictions, social workers have core on-the-job-training first, shadow an experienced worker, and are eased into responsibility for specific cases. In British Columbia, for example, there is now a four-month training programme for new staff, which is one result of the inquiry into child protection services in that province[12].

Social workers are trained to practice skills such as getting to know clients, going through the story of a problem together, including asking what went wrong, when it happened, who was involved, what has been tried with what results, what would be useful, and so forth, agreeing on steps for problem-solving. But good social work practice is a process which requires time and resources which they do not generally have. Some expressed the feeling of being in a 'Catch-22 situation'. They do not have time to do the casework and counselling, which are now increasingly being contracted out to others, and changing their own role to one that is less involved in direct practice. Consequently, they are finding that they are losing skills necessary for doing their work.

Mi'kmaq Family and Children's Services (MFCS). In this First Nations agency, the staff also identified resources as the most critical issue facing them in their child welfare work. They see child welfare in the context of community development, and do not divorce it from the struggles of their people for self-government and to improve their economic and social conditions.

MFCS staff emphasise the preventive aspects of their child welfare mandate by visiting families as soon as possible after hearing of problems. Because Mi'kmaq communities are smaller in population and physical size in comparison to rest of the Halifax metropolitan area, and because they share historical and cultural traditions and experiences of oppression, the Mi'kmaq people know each other better and are more aware of personal and family difficulties when these occur. Relatives and neighbours are likely to help each other and to alert agency staff about problems as they arise. Staff can then visit on a more informal basis to talk with family members and to see what help may be needed to resolve difficulties before they become emergencies.

In spite of under-funding, large caseloads and inadequate resources, the staff try to work with families as long as possible before going to court. They see legal procedures as a last resort, that does not generally further the helping process. By going to court, the relationships between social workers and family members change, because both are forced to take more adversarial and polarised positions. If staff have to bring a parent or family before a judge, they delay asking for permanent care for as long as possible to give the family and social workers time to mobilise supports and strengths needed to provide care for the children.

When Mi'kmaq children have to be removed from their parents' care on a temporary or longer-term basis, they move to the homes of relatives or neighbours within their same communities or with family members who live on a different reserve. Even if this move is carried out under the auspices of the MFCS' foster care programme, it is not as traumatic for the children and their parents as moving to an unknown foster home. Children may move among parents, grandparents, other family members and friends and feel and be 'home'. In the view of MFCS staff, the notion of permanency in child care is more invested in communities and extended families than in individual parents.

A strong emphasis on shared community and social work values, forms a foundation upon which staff feel they can struggle against obstacles to good social work practice being imposed by insufficient resources, difficult work and legal processes. MFCS staff feel that their philosophy and approaches are rooted in Mi'kmaq history, values, culture, and current social conditions, and that their ideas and methods could be useful in governmental and more traditional child welfare agencies. They expressed a desire to share their practice methods and explore differences with social workers in government and private child welfare agencies, but have felt some tension when they have tried to do so. They feel their ideas may be dismissed because of differences between their agency and mainstream services. Conditions are sometimes perceived as so different that what works for one agency would not be seen as working in others.

2. *How have Financial Restraints Affected your Work in Providing Child Welfare Services?*

Since much information about the effects of cutbacks was provided in response to the question about critical issues, this section will be limited to a summary of the points made during our interviews. Decreased funding and fewer staff in relation to the amount of work, and the severity and complexity of personal and family problems, mean that social workers have higher caseloads and fewer government and community-based support services. Supervisory, secretarial, and other support staff have not increased in relation to the volume and changes in the nature of the work. One change of significance is the greatly increased requirement for documentation and reporting in child protection services, which increases the work of all personnel in the child welfare system. When the provincial government increases money for staffing, it specifies in what positions staff are to be hired; as a result, most often agencies are required to hire social workers to fill front-line positions rather than supervisory or support staff.

Fiscal cutbacks and the restructuring of social programmes have resulted in a downloading of cases from health and education to community services and then to child protection services. With the closure of residential facilities for children with intellectual disabilities, for example, child welfare agencies are often expected to find placements for these children with special needs. Such placements do not yet exist and money has not been available to date to develop community-based alternatives to institutional care. Similarly, fewer beds are available for adolescents who require treatment for mental health problems or group homes. In fact, services for young people from sixteen to nineteen years of age have long been recognised as severely limited. Child welfare agencies have to take cases that would have been handled by special institutions or health facilities, even though the resources for children and youth with special needs are underdeveloped or lacking altogether. Social workers who already feel overworked, stressed, and undervalued are required to do even more work without the necessary specialised resources.

Increasing caseloads and decreasing resources means that the work becomes more and more driven by emergencies, and more crisis management than systematic problem solving, adding to stress and dissatisfaction with the job.

3. What would be Most Useful to You and Your Agency in Your Efforts to Improve the Quality of Child Welfare Services?

In keeping with what they had identified as critical issues, the staff interviewed listed funding for more staff and a range of resources to provide the care required by children and their families as the things that would be most helpful. They are all too aware that most of the parents and families they work with are poor, most often lone-parent women, who are managing under worsening conditions that result from cuts in social welfare programmes, unemployment or low wages, and lack of education and job training, and who also have to cope with a variety of problems such as violence, addiction and mental illness. The economic and social conditions of clients of child welfare are fairly well-known and are documented in many government reports and academic studies[13].

Second to resources was the concern about the changing practice in child welfare. Staff felt that social workers need to deal more effectively with the inherent conflict in child welfare between helping families and investigating allegations of child neglect and abuse, between the role of counsellor, support person, and advocate, and that of apprehending children[14]. Staff interviewed also expressed the need to examine and redefine social work practice in child welfare in today's circumstances, emphasising the traditional aspects of helping, counselling, supporting, and advocating. Social workers in child welfare, perhaps through their professional associations and organisations, ought to examine the practice of social work, determine what it is and what it should be, and assert that definition more powerfully.

Specific suggestions for increasing social work knowledge and skills included court training. Social workers need more training in how to articulate their views strongly in court, and more generally, in how to explain and defend their positions with others who are more powerful in governments, other professions, the media and elsewhere[15]. As one worker said: 'We are experiencing profound changes in our work and we are not saying enough about these in places where it counts.'

In view of the increasing diversity of their clients, colleagues and the general population, social workers need more training in cross-cultural practice. They feel that they are sensitive to racial and cultural diversity, but have not received sufficient training in this area to meet the demands of their practice. They need to build on their present awareness by learning, for example, how to respond to racism or accusations of racism, and how to deal with conflict in polarised situations.

Improvements in working conditions, the third major concern raised and one not separate from social work practice, will require some form of collective action through unions where these exist, or through workplace action.

Staff felt they are too immersed in their daily work and too busy to keep up with reading, and suggested ways to keep up to date with developments in their field. One suggestion was for an ongoing programme of presentations on developments in practice, social policy and research in forms that practitioners can use. Another idea was that the Maritime School of Social Work and agencies could engage in joint research in areas such as the impact of financial cuts and programme changes on child welfare practice. Additionally, these studies could identify and disseminate examples of 'best practice', that is, case examples of what kinds of approaches are useful in specific situations, and why.

Some staff expressed the idea that if people were better informed and understood the lives of clients, they could support the allocation of more resources to child welfare. Others questioned public commitment to child welfare, saying that a great deal of information on poverty, unemployment, drug dependency, and homelessness is already available. Staff wondered why some members of the public remain uninformed and, if the public is already informed, why are there not adequate resources and why is there no public outcry.

Summary and Implications

Findings from preliminary meetings with staff in child welfare agencies indicate that they cannot achieve the goals of child protection because budgetary constraints and the ways that monies are allocated for the implementation of child welfare responsibilities constrain their efforts in this regard. Underfunding means agencies have fewer staff members than are required and caseloads are considerably higher than the recommended standard. As a consequence, staff work is directed towards crises and cases that are assessed to be 'high risk'. With the exception of the MFCS, prevention services are not being adequately addressed.

Changes in legislation and in the structure of funding have also brought about profound changes in the nature of social work practice in child welfare. Courts more often require that psychological and social assessments and counselling, the heart of social work, be done by professionals in private practice, rather than by child welfare workers assigned to the case. Social workers have become more like case managers, seeing that court-ordered services are carried out and recorded.

Child welfare workers have experienced a loss of power to define and do their own work. High caseloads, changes in legislation and legal processes are determining what they are able to do to protect children and assist families. Personal safety, liability for child abuse and death, and working conditions are emerging as critical issues in child welfare. Not surprisingly, child welfare workers are experiencing a loss in job satisfaction, increased stress and burnout.

In spite of the profound changes in their work and the serious difficulties they face, the child welfare staff we interviewed expressed a sense of the importance of their work. The knowledge that they and their services made a positive difference in the lives of some children and their families helped to sustain them in their work. They were also able to gather support from one another and from team meetings at their various offices.

Resources and changes in practice were named as the two most critical issues facing child welfare staff. Although under-funding of child welfare is a chronic problem, it has recently become more acute and resulted in deteriorating services and working conditions. There is a sense of being immersed and overwhelmed by problems and of not knowing how to solve them, a sense of crisis.

Differences between larger metropolitan agencies and the Mi'kmaq Family and Children's Services appear to be significant. Further exploration would be useful to understand more about how MFCS staff practice prevention, manage their relations with lawyers and courts, and organise their work. Factors mentioned included the agency's formation as a distinct service to Mi'kmaq communities, its role in the process of achieving self-government, and its roots in the history, traditions, and current social conditions of Mi'kmaq communities. It is also a newer agency, less entrenched in bureaucracy, flatter in organisational form, and located in rural areas. It would be useful to do further interviews with staff at agencies which are located in rural and small town areas and to compare their views and experiences with those from both the metropolitan and Mi'kmaq child welfare agencies in order to see what can be learned.

The primary goals of the international project, *Child Abuse, Protection and Welfare*, are to facilitate the exchange of students for field placements and to build child welfare curricula within an international context. As a result of this Project, we hope to learn more about how child welfare work is being practised in the participating countries, whether problems and issues are similar, and how these can be addressed. In light of the preliminary work we have done, it seems clear that social work theory and practice in child welfare require a fundamental re-examination based on the current conditions in the field. Engaging in this re-examination and reshaping curricula are challenges, but they are also essential to take on for the benefit of children, their families, and social work itself.

Notes

1   The other schools of social work are at Southampton University (U.K.), Hogeschool West-Brabant (Netherlands), Stockholm University (Sweden), the University of Victoria (Canada) and   McMaster University (Canada). Dalhousie University is located in Halifax, Nova Scotia, Canada.

2   Members of the project team at Dalhousie's Maritime School of Social Work are Wanda Thomas Bernard, Joan Gilroy, Marilyn Peers and Gwendolyn MacDonald Slipp. These faculty represent a range of scholarly, educational and professional interests which include the development of a curriculum in social work which includes an analysis of social inequality based on factors such as gender, 'race', culture, disability, sexual orientation, and poverty.
      We are grateful to the staff members who met with us to discuss the project and current issues in child welfare work.

3   For an overview of the welfare policies of Canada's provincial and territorial governments, see: *Another Look at Welfare Reform,* The National Council of Welfare, Ottawa, Minister of Public Works and Government Services Canada, 1977.

4   The Parliament of Canada set a goal of eliminating child poverty by the year 2000. Standing Committee on Health and Welfare, Social Affairs, Seniors and the Status of Women, *Towards 2000: Eliminating Child Poverty,* Ottawa, Queen's Printer, 1993.

5   Information about child welfare and residential services provided by the Nova Scotia Department of Community Services can be obtained from its website at http://www.gov.ns.ca/coms/child.htm.

6   The *Children and Family Services Act, Statutes of Nova Scotia,* Chapter 5, 1990, Halifax, Queen's Printer, 1990 and *Children and Family Services Regulations, 1995,* Halifax, Queen's Printer, 1995.

7   Letters to the provincial Director of Child Welfare, the provincial Administrator of Family and Children's Services, the supervisors of three provincial child welfare offices in metropolitan Halifax, the Executive Director of the CAS of Halifax, and the Executive Director of the MFCS invited them, together with a member of their supervisory and front-line staff, to a meeting at the Maritime School of Social Work (MSSW).

8   The purposes of this meeting have been stated above.
      In the first meeting, held at the MSSW in September, all four faculty team members met with six staff members. One of the staff was a front-line worker and five were supervisors or managers. All six worked in provincial child welfare offices located in the metropolitan region. Since it was not possible to find one day in which staff from all the agencies could meet, we scheduled subsequent meetings separately with MFCS and Halifax CAS staff. Two Project team members met with MFCS staff and two with CAS; both meetings were held in the agencies' offices in October, 1997. In total, three separate meetings were held with eleven staff members, most of whom were administrators and supervisors.
      Discussions in these meetings focused on the three questions posed in the letter of invitation about critical issues, financial restraints, and possibilities for

improving child welfare services. All four team members were involved in at least one meeting; and, one member was present for all meetings. This same member conducted the separate interviews with two graduate students, both of whom had worked in child protection for a considerable number of years (four and a half and ten and a half years in two provinces, Nova Scotia and British Columbia) and a telephone interview with a third graduate student who had some experience doing contract work with a private agency.

9 Here I am referring to newsletters put out by the Maritime School of Social Work, the Nova Scotia Association of Social Workers and the Nova Scotia Council for the Family, where students, members of the professional association, and child welfare staff would be likely to see the information about this project.

10 The Child Welfare League of America (CWLA) and the Child Welfare League of Canada (CWLC) establish standards in caseload size and other matters, make policy recommendations, and engage in research and advocacy. The CWLC was newly incorporated in affiliation with the CWLA, to which Canadian child welfare agencies have long belonged. The provincial Department of Community Services also establishes standards in the area of child protection which are published in policy manuals, for example, in its child protection services policy manual dated January, 1996.

11 Canadian Association of Social Workers Social Work Code of Ethics (1994) and Nova Scotia Association of Social Workers Amendments (1994).

12 The *Report of the Gove Inquiry into Child Protection in British Columbia, 1995*, by the Honorable Thomas J. Gove, Commissioner, Province of British Columbia.

13 See, for example, *Changing the Child Welfare Agenda: Contributions from Canada; A Special Issue of Child Welfare,* edited by S. Scarth, B. Wharf, and E. Tyrwhitt, vol. LXXIV, no. 3, May/June, 1995; 'Manufacturing 'Bad Mothers': A Critical Perspective on Child Neglect' by K.J. Swift, University of Toronto Press, Toronto, 1995; *Rethinking Child Welfare in Canada,* edited by B. Wharf, Toronto, McClelland and Stewart, 1993; and numerous publications by the National Council on Welfare and the Canadian Council on Social Development.

14 Wharf (1993, pp. 218-220) recommends that investigations of child neglect and abuse be done by family courts because investigations are incompatible with the role of helper. Social workers would then be able to focus on providing support for parents and helping them obtain the resources they require. For further information, refer to *Rethinking Child Welfare in Canada,* edited by B. Wharf, McClelland and Stewart, Toronto, 1993.

15 Swift (1995, pp. 486-502) discusses the gendered nature of the struggle for power and influence in child welfare between law and social work, and

examines obstacles to redefining practice in the context of a feminist analysis of women's work. Calling women in child welfare 'missing persons,' she suggests that directions for change include the transformation of child welfare by feminist theory and practice which includes 'race' and class as central. 'Missing Persons: Women in Child Welfare,' by K. Swift in *Changing the Child Welfare Agenda: Contributions from Canada,* edited by S. Scarth, B. Wharf and E. Tyrwhitt

References

Gove, T.J. (1995), *The Report of the Gove Inquiry into Child Protection in British Columbia,* Province of British Columbia, Victoria.

National Council of Welfare (1977), *Another Look at Welfare Reform,* Minister of Public and Government Services Canada, Ottawa.

Scarth, S., Wharf, B. and Tyrwhittt, E. (eds) (1995a), *A Special Issue of Child Welfare,* vol. LXXIV, no. 3, May/June, pp. 486-502.

Scarth, S., Wharf, B. and Tyrwhitt, E. (eds) (1995b), *Changing the Child Welfare Agenda: Contributions from Canada,* University of Toronto Press, Toronto.

Swift, K.J. (1995), 'Manufacturing 'Bad Mothers': A Critical Perspective on Child Neglect', in S. Scarth, B. Wharf and E. Tyrwhitt (eds), *Changing the Child Welfare Agenda: Contributions from Canada,* University of Toronto Press, Toronto.

Wharf, B. (1993), *Rethinking Child Welfare in Canada,* McClelland and Stewart, Inc., Toronto.

3 Creating Second-class Citizens in Child Welfare

MARILYN CALLAHAN

Introduction

Contemporary debates about child welfare policy and practice proceed along two dimensions: protection, child-centred approach on one hand versus the prevention and family-centred approach on the other. On one side are those who believe that the mandate of child welfare should be a narrow one, involving only those few families whose care for their children is clearly substandard and should focus, first and foremost, on the protection and rights of children. Prevention and family-centred advocates are those that believe that the family is the unit of service in child welfare and families should be assisted to care for children long before serious difficulties arise. Of course, others argue that child welfare should be concerned about both family and child, prevention and protection and in fact, these aims represent a continuum rather than mutually exclusive positions.

While the dominant discourse in child welfare is framed in the above debates, there are other points of view which receive less notice. Structural analysts suggest that child welfare will never make gains within a child or family service framework. They argue convincingly for changes in major family policies to promote greater income equality, work force participation of women and improved housing, health and education systems (Moreau and Leonard, 1989). While this analysis makes sense to many, it offers little to harried workers in their day-to-day practice.

Feminists have contributed to child welfare thinking in several important ways. They have unravelled both the oppression and opportunity inherent in child welfare services (Gordon, 1986), taken aim at the reinforcement of inequality within child welfare based upon gender, 'race' and class (Mason, 1993; Hutchison, 1992; Parton and Parton, 1989) and fostered an understanding of violence amongst family members, including women and their children, as taking place within the context of a patriarchal culture (Thorpe, 1996). They promote changes which resemble structural reforms at the grand level but which also include an emphasis on the role of women in caregiving. Further, they suggest practice changes within the daily work of child welfare which redress the power imbalances inherent in the work (Thorpe, 1993; Smith and Smith, 1990; Swift,1991,1995; Krane, 1994). This analysis holds great promise for child welfare because it attempts to design changes in short term practice which are consistent with and support the vision for larger scale reforms. However, as yet feminist thinking is not widely embraced in child welfare.

The intent of this article is to build on the work of structural and feminist approaches through the insights gained from research with women/mothers and their child welfare workers. I argue that contemporary debates about prevention and protection, family-centred or child-centred have been constructed primarily by academics and professionals without focusing on the experience of clients and front line workers. The findings from the research indicate that another issue occupies their concerns: participants including women/mothers and social workers, experience themselves as second class citizens. The services that they receive and give in child welfare, rather than ameliorate this situation, often reinforces their second class status. I conclude with another approach to child welfare, one that embraces some of the protection-prevention dialogue but argues for the promotion of citizenship as a more useful aim for child welfare.

The Research Project

Much of the material for this article is based upon research carried out with a government child welfare agency over the past five years in British Columbia, Canada. This statutory child welfare programme is decentralised from provincial headquarters to many local offices throughout the province and charged with the full gamut of services including child protection, family support, adoptions and foster care. Although results of the first phase of the project have been reported earlier

46

(Callahan and Lumb, 1995) this article includes some of the findings from the second phase where five new centres in different parts of the province joined the research (Callahan and Wharf, 1995; Herringer and Isaac, 1996). The research question was a simple one: 'What happens when women/mothers involved in child welfare and their workers are asked to design and carry out their own approaches to child welfare?' We were interested not only in the outcomes of their work but the process that unfolded as they worked together.

Single parent women most of whom had been reported to child welfare authorities for their seemingly inadequate care of their children constituted one group of participants in the project. This group was selected because they represent the majority of individuals served by child welfare programmes. Front-line child welfare workers, mostly women with varying degrees of experience and education, also participated in the project. The two groups met separately and together to discuss their differing experiences in child welfare. Within these conversations and the resulting actions came the impetus for much of our own re-thinking about child welfare.

The research method was an adaptation of participatory action research. The research questions was formulated by the researchers but, beyond that, the participants were free to proceed as they wished. Of course, participants were restricted in their actions in several important ways. Workers were still employees of a government agency and had to work within the broad policy guidelines of that organisation, including the mandate to remove children from their homes. Their own caseloads were high and they often felt that they had little time or inclination to ponder the meaning of their work. Women/mothers had modest resources as almost all were in receipt of income assistance from the same government department. Many were suspicious of child welfare personnel. Like workers, their lives were very busy and contemplation was a luxury most could not afford.

The Findings

Although the process of the projects unfolded differently in various offices, some patterns were common. After agreeing to participate, child welfare workers met with the researchers over a period of several months to express their own frustrations with their jobs and to talk about how these could be done differently. For some staff, the prospects of creating change in their work were remote. They believed that they could not add one more thing to their already hectic schedule, nor could they be expected to think creatively when they had always been instructed to follow a plethora of specific policy guidelines. To help alleviate some of these difficulties, one worker was designated as the project co-ordinator, often for several offices, and was freed from most of her regular duties for the duration of the project.

Organising the women/mothers was equally challenging. In the initial stage, the project co-ordinators received referrals from other workers and identified likely participants from their own caseloads. After initial meetings usually held in the child welfare office, women were encouraged to invite others. Early conversations in these groups were similar to those which took place in the workers' groups. Women/mothers described their daily lives, the hard work of raising children in poverty, the effort involved in receiving help and their own personal concerns. Over time, the realisation of their shared situation encouraged many to think of the group as a source of support and strength. While some women/mothers were unable to continue participation primarily because of their own crisis situation, most remained and left only after they obtained work or went back to school.

In some offices, these groups continued to meet separately, in others, the groups began meetings together to explore possible changes in service. Coming together was not a smooth process. Some women/mothers were very angry and used the opportunity of joint meetings to express their pain and frustration about child welfare to the workers at hand. Some workers had difficulty speaking collegially to women/mothers and to listen to their realities. However, from these deliberations emerged some highly creative activities, described briefly in turn.

a. Consciousness Raising Regarding the Work and Lives of Mothers and Workers

Many of the conversations of workers and women/mothers meeting alone and together raised awareness about the similarities of their daily lives. Although some women knew each other before and had discussed these issues in twos and threes, many women had kept their struggles to themselves and were surprised that others felt the same way they did. This was as true for the workers as the women/mothers. These struggles were many but two major insights emerged from these conversations. The first occurred primarily within the discussions of women/mothers: that their daily responsibilities in caring for children constituted work. Most women had not thought of their contributions as work and had not been encouraged to do so. Indeed, they were categorised as 'unemployable' or 'unemployed' by their welfare workers. Yet, as they talked about their daily lives and the barriers set up by agency policies, they realised that they carried out complex tasks and overcame substantial adversities.

The development of this awareness proceeded haphazardly in the discussion. For instance, one woman described her daily routine caring for a handicapped child and two other children in a rural area with an unreliable car. When she requested assistance with car insurance and repairs, she was given short shrift by her worker who suggested she ferry her children in a buggy to their school, several miles away. The group digested this story in several stages: first laughing at the ignorance of a paid worker who did not consider the humiliation of a child arriving at school in a baby buggy and the sheer impossibility for a woman to negotiate such an onerous trip at least four times a day, as if she had nothing else to do. Then they wondered why workers and others thought that they had nothing to do, why their activities were so unknown. Next, they talked about the delivery of social, education and health services which made their days even more complicated: the welfare office over here, the child and family services over there, the doctor here, the physiotherapist in yet another corner of the community. It dawned on many that their work involved not only raising children but getting necessary subsistence and services from organisations set up for the convenience of others, not themselves. Moreover, they had to deal with many different people in order to get a simple service or fend off a prying agency. Child welfare work was so specialised that often five or six different individuals would be involved with a busy mother at any one time.

Over time the conversation included the very specific details of how to extract the right kind of service from recalcitrant workers and unsympathetic policies. Women described the best 'client' stance: persistent but polite, offering solutions not just problems, being grateful and subservient. Group members also described their humiliation as they adopt survival practices which belittled themselves. To be a successful client, women had to balance their image carefully: pathetic enough to merit help yet competent enough to keep her children.

The second major insight involved understanding stigma and its impact. Over and over, women told stories about what it felt like to be reported by neighbours for supposedly neglecting or abusing their children, of being humiliated in the grocery line when they had to use a food voucher, of the suffering of their children because they could not afford to give them appropriate clothes and social activities. One woman described her month long effort to find money for a cub uniform for her son: approaching her worker, being referred to a service club, making her needs known to others in the community and finally being late with the money, much to her son's embarrassment. Workers also described their feelings of alienation. Often they did not mention to others that they were social workers in child welfare to avoid diatribes about people on welfare or comments such as 'I don't how can you stand it, I never could'.

While feelings of stigma corroded self-esteem, they also kept women quiet and isolated, contributing to the general ignorance about their work and their struggles. The conversations about stigma did not stop with sharing stories. Women wondered why they should be so derided and began to speculate about who is considered a 'good' mother - only those who are married to an employed man or who support themselves. The care of the children seemed to merit less importance than the source of the income for that care. The hypocrisy of governments and communities which talk about their concern for children but refuse resources to ensure good care was also noted.

b. Self-help Initiatives

Not surprisingly some women decided to use their newly discovered commonalities as a base for efforts to change their circumstances. For women/mothers, the self-help efforts focused on improving their economic situation and their feelings of personal and family safety. These were priorities. Such efforts as a community garden, a clothing exchange, the start of a small business, child care co-operatives and so forth, spoke directly to their financial needs. Given that child welfare is predominately a 'poor people's service' this action is not surprising. The degree of violence experienced by these women is also well-known but often overlooked in child welfare. Many women were in or had experienced violent relationships and were knowledgeable about self-protection. Nonetheless, they were surprised that other women were handling similar problems. Over time, some groups developed action strategies. For instance, one woman complained about an ex-partner who parked his truck in her driveway, in spite of a court order that he not enter her premises. The empty truck served as a reminder of his continuing presence, although the police said that they could not intervene unless he actually entered her home or harmed her in some way. The group of women/mothers decided to take action, writing a letter to the man informing him that they were aware of his activities and watching over their friend. The truck disappeared.

Self-help for workers took many forms including a group of young workers who met to discuss the difficulties of their lives in an unfamiliar northern region. Turnover was high in this region and others that serve areas far from large urban cities in British Columbia. The reasons for the turnover were not surprising as women described their personal and professional lives. Feelings of lack of safety and social isolation predominated and were often exacerbated by workplace policies. The essential contribution of this and other self-help efforts focused upon creating a different way of relating to each other within work groups and across agencies, creating different forms of collegial relationships based upon trust and voluntary participation.

c.   *Social Action Groupwork on Issues Affecting both Workers and Women/Mothers*

In an earlier article, Callahan and Lumb (1994) reported on the development of social action groupwork within the first phase of the project which became a prominent feature of the second phase as well. Essentially, social action groupwork differs from self-help activities in that it joins workers and clients together on actions which concern both with a focus on changing policies and services (Mullander and Ward, 1991). For instance, clients and workers both benefited from the challenge to policy which did not authorise day care benefits for those mothers in day treatment for alcohol and drug abuse. Workers were discouraged when women did not stay in treatment because they found treatment too difficult without home help. Similarly, the retention of more of their maintenance payments prior to the reduction in welfare payments was a concern for both workers and clients. In this instance, they took issue with the policy and prepared an analysis with alternatives based upon the realities of women raising children alone. Interestingly, social action groupwork also involved promoting individual women and workers for membership on key decision making bodies. One women was nominated for a newly formed provincial review panel regarding children in care. In another, workers became active in their union.

d.   *Community Development and Education*

Closely related to social action groupwork were community development activities. One stream of activity concentrated on the creation of resources to benefit women - a welfare information centre, a women's centre, an advisory council for a child welfare office, a single parent association. These activities involved workers, women/mothers, other community organisations and interested citizens in mutual campaigns and actions. Another focus for community development work was educational initiatives which challenged stereotypes about poor single mothers and the people who work with them. Examples of these endeavours included articles for the daily press regarding women's lives and an invitation to family court judges to listen to the concerns of both workers and clients about family court.

e.   *Life Changes*

Without doubt, the workers and women/mothers who participated in various aspects of the project came away with some significant changes in their perspectives. Some workers were clear that they did not wish to practice in this fashion. While in a minority, they made their views known. A few quit child welfare practice. Their departure was not acrimonious as they realised that they were either not suited for such a shift in their practice or they were simply worn-out. Most workers prospered under this approach to practice and experienced considerable renewal. The co-ordinators reported substantial benefit and longed to continue in their position after the official project ended.

Changes which women/mothers made to their lives was considerable. Some women, probably the majority, had never had any sense of their own collective power and knowledge. This feeling coupled with a demystification of the knowledge of professionals and other community members gave them the courage to go back to school, take jobs, take leadership positions in the organisations which they had founded, and so forth. They reported that their capacity to parent improved as well. Not only did they feel better about themselves and have the support of others, but they were also far better consumers of services. They knew what services were available and how to access them.

While each of these activities have been reported separately in the above discussion, most often, several occurred at once within one meeting or activity. For instance, near the end of the project, two researchers attended a steering committee meeting for several sites, where workers and women/mothers met to provide a summary of activities. When it came time to give the workers' report, an experienced worker began to describe the tremendous changes occurring in the organisation because of new legislation and policy. She talked about how staff were stressed and worn out with all the confusion. At that point, a new member, a woman whose children had been removed from her home and who suffered from addictions, unemployment and many other difficulties, broke in.

She told the group that the stresses of social workers hardly matched those of herself and others like her. In a voice trembling with anger and despair she described what had happened to her and how she feared that she could never get her children back. In fact, while she had tried to do what the worker demanded of her, get counselling for a start, even that effort had failed. The family counselling centre where she was referred had a long waiting list and could not take her for three months. At that point, she began weeping. The social worker fell silent. Several other women entered the conversation, making practical suggestions about what the woman could do next, such as declare an emergency at the family counselling centre and thus go to the top of the waiting list. As the conversation proceeded, women talked about how important it was to have their own plan about recovery and share it with the worker, rather than taking a passive stance. Several offered to help the new member with a realistic and meaningful plan and to come with her to see her worker, an offer that was accepted. The conversation turned to the whole notion of taking charge rather than positioning oneself as a victim, workers and clients alike. Suggestions about the need to develop groups to help women in similar circumstances were proposed. Some women/mothers explained how social workers felt many of the same frustrations as they did. The business meeting continued.

Rethinking Child Welfare

The experience of women and their workers in re-designing child welfare raises some fundamental questions about conceptions of child welfare. Time after time, participants described a child welfare system that undermined their confidence and made them feel like 'second class citizens'. These remarks pertained to the receipt of family support services as well as protective and investigatory ones. While workers were in a better position compared to women/mothers, they also spoke about being on the bottom of the heap in their organisations and professional communities. Some mentioned that they would never even tell their neighbours what they did for a living. An understanding of how women experience second class citizenship and how policies and practices construct and reinforce this status was a crucial finding of the project. Embedded within the above activities, are the essential elements of citizenship to these women. These elements emerged from the discussions with participants and are considered in the analysis which follows. These indicate the importance of having further debate on the subject of citizenship. Another step in analysis, beyond the scope of this paper, is to compare these with elements identified by others, particularly those engaged in debates about changing definitions of citizenship (Brodie,1996; Kymlicka, 1992).

Economic Well Being

First and foremost, it was clear that citizenship to these women means having sufficient economic resources and being recognised as a valued worker. Many activities within the project focused upon improving family resources and acknowledging women's work in the home and community. The community garden, clothing exchanges and media efforts to promote understanding of the struggles of single parents, spoke to these needs.

The extent to which child welfare does not deal with the poverty of most of their clients is well known (Pelton,1978; Magura and Moses, 1984). What is less acknowledged are the processes by which child welfare services actually maintain and even increase the poverty of their clients. The first contacts between child welfare workers and clients usually focus upon the inadequate care which mothers are providing. While lack of resources may be the central reason why mothers are struggling, child welfare services are not designed to increase resources. Instead, they are fashioned to improve the capacity of parents to cope in the face of poverty. Thus, parenting programmes, counselling, drug and alcohol treatment centres and so forth, all address the individual, psychological 'problems' of parents, as defined by others. Refusing such services means running the risk of losing children to child welfare agencies and thus parents, already working hard to cope in poor circumstances, must work even harder to 'get better'. Some of the services are delivered in their own home, others must be reached by public transportation or walking, often in different directions in the community. For many women, the prospects of finding paid work outside the home after contact with child welfare authorities were dimmed. Not only do they risk further criticism of their parenting, they simply have less time and reduced confidence in themselves.

Should parents lose their children, then they often become poorer, as maintenance and welfare payments are reduced. Yet, in order to have children returned to them, they must be able to demonstrate that they have a home and resources to support them. One woman described her struggle after her child was placed in a psychiatric facility in another community. Not only did she lose her support payments for the child, she had to attend family counselling sessions at the facility to demonstrate that she was capable of having the child returned. Gas, car insurance, tires, meals, child care for her daughter at home, consumed many resources. Yet, she had to explain to her worker why she needed extra expenses 'when her child was not at home'.

While all of this is occurring, the actual work which mothers are already carrying out is not recognised, indeed, it is the focus of concern. The women in this project revealed how their work is made invisible - someone expresses a complaint about the care of their children which is translated into an investigation into their adequacy as mothers and then into treatment to improve their psychological capability and moral strength as women. What they are actually doing day by day and perhaps doing well is never the subject of the inquiry.

Child welfare workers face a similar sense that their work is not valued. Most entered social work with the intention of helping others. Yet, few seem to benefit from their work nor, do many appreciate their efforts. Those of us in the research team were disheartened to learn the extent to which child welfare workers felt isolated. Not only did their clients not want to see them, but they also felt under suspicion by management who appeared to distrust their judgement, and were alienated by other professionals who seemed disappointed in their inability to address child abuse and neglect.

Reciprocity

A second dimension to citizenship was the right to be a part of a community and contribute to its well-being. A strong theme in the discussion and activities of participants was the desire to improve not only their situation and their children's lives but to help others. Most activities in the project were characterised by a strong sense of reciprocity. Women/mothers helped each other and social workers, providing advice, insights into their lives, suggested improvements in policy and practice and practical consumer information about social services. Workers gave help as well, teaching women/mothers about resources, policies, and their own circumstances.

The project illuminated how present child welfare services exclude clients from reciprocal relationships. Cast as poor mothers from the outset, and seen by workers on an individual basis, women understand that the aim of services is to improve their functioning with time limited services so that they can continue on their own. The notion that a capable parent is one that does not need ongoing support is instilled from the beginning. Moreover, clients are not encouraged to meet one another, see how others may be in the same boat and identify their extensive knowledge in manoeuvring through the complex web of services and policies.

From the inception of services, reciprocity between workers and clients is discouraged. The one designated to investigate the other is placed in a distant and superior role. Interestingly, although women/mothers described the caring and helpful actions of workers in the face of their difficult job, they did not identify any instances where they felt that they had helped the worker. Only through joint meetings did they become aware of the pleasure that workers feel when they achieve more egalitarian relationships with their clients. Altogether, child welfare services encourage women to shape their identity as receivers and consumers rather than as those who contribute to the well being of others and the community.

Justice

A third characteristic of citizenship is related to the desire for justice. While fair legal processes were important to women, the need for justice extended much further than the courtroom. Women spoke frequently about being at sea with professional services: not understanding the rules which were unpublished and having to depend upon the grace and favour of workers. In such situations, they described how they felt like supplicants and were unable to plan for themselves or protest the quality or range of services. Many of the activities in the project were designed to remedy this situation including a client resource room, pamphlets on available services and self-help groups.

Workers reported a similar sense that clear and reliable information was impossible to obtain. The policy directives contained in a plethora of manuals were constantly changing and were often unhelpful and unrealistic, yet, they ignored them at their peril. Workers expressed their own anxiety about the audit system where inspectors arrived to examine their files and check on their work.

Participation

A fourth component of citizenship is one that it most connected to the usual definition of citizen: the right to vote and have a say in one's major life decisions. Women/mothers talked extensively about their inability to affect decisions in child welfare. If they pushed for input, they risked appearing aggressive. If they accepted what happened to them, they were left feeling ineffective. The decision-making opportunities open to them were often framed within a narrow band of choices: whether they voluntarily admitted their children to care or went to court; which facility was most appropriate for their child; which support programme amongst a list they preferred; and so forth. The real decisions: whether to have the child welfare officials involved in their family or not; which worker they preferred; and how they defined help; were not open to them.

The central aim of this project was to place women and workers in decision-making roles. They were able to design the work as they saw fit and to participate or not as they wished. Some workers struggled with this freedom and admitted candidly that they experienced both exhilaration and vulnerability. It was easier to carry out practice as before, seeing individual clients, being in charge (at least in the office) about what happened. However, workers also expressed the need to have more influence on child welfare policy and made the connections between their situation and that of their clients. They stated that policy made in headquarters by officials far away from the front-line workers who are expected to carry them out were often as irrelevant as the decisions workers foisted on clients.

Safety

A fifth component of citizenship for these participants was a fundamental one: the right to be safe in their homes and communities. Traditional conceptions of citizenship focus upon safety. In fact, a defining role of the state has been to protect its citizens from attack. In this project, we were disheartened to learn about the lack of safety experienced by many women/mothers and workers. Most women/mothers had experienced violence in their relationships with their spouses and other partners or at least a lack of security regarding the relationship. Many women were grappling with constant fear as a regular part of their lives. Workers felt unsafe as well. They knew that if they made a mistake, or at least if the press or management deemed their work in error, that they were likely to face censure or even dismissal. Workers also discussed the fear that they sometimes experienced, particularly as women, when entering situations of potential and actual violence.

One of the results of the collective action in this project was the opportunity to discuss safety as a central issue and to feel the support of others in tackling it. However, traditional child welfare work often exacerbates the feelings of vulnerability of women and workers. Investigations by child welfare workers contribute to further unsettling women and their families. Suddenly, a new dimension is added to their lives: fear of losing their children; fear of being discovered inadequate; fear of losing their income; and so forth. Child welfare, as a individual case-by-case activity often places workers in unsafe situations. While workers frequently work in teams and with police, unexpected situations arise where they feel vulnerable, particularly in the homes of their clients.

Belonging

The final component of citizenship is perhaps the most elusive and yet the most crucial - the need to belong and be valued as a whole person. Much of the time in this project was spent on this issue: the right to be valued as women, not just as mothers, and as women equal to other citizens, not as faulty, low-class women draining the public purse. Robert Pinker, in his classic text, *Social Theory and Social Policy*, underlines the connection between stigma, or the lack of a feeling of belonging, and citizenship. He argues that:

> in any system of exchange, self respect and the respect of others is maintained by the ability to make some return for what is received. Stigma - the denial of citizenship - attaches most firmly to those whose dependency is either prolonged or self induced (Pinker, 1971, p. 157).

Women/mothers in child welfare fit Pinker's (1971) requirements for a stigmatised group. They are cast as women who do not give return for what they receive. Indeed, the ideology of motherhood holds that women do not need instruction or even support to fulfil their mothering tasks. According to this view, women requiring such assistance, particularly by the state, are taking what they should not need. Women/mothers are also portrayed as having got into this pickle by themselves. They should have chosen a husband who would provide for and care about his family; otherwise they should not have had children. Further, they should have been able to protect their children from the violence in the home and the ravages of poverty. And, there is a prevailing view that these women and their children will need help for protracted periods of time, given their meagre personal and financial resources.

Concluding Remarks

I began this article with the comment that the current debates in child welfare: protection versus prevention and child-centred versus family-centred do not reflect the reality of client and worker's experience. I used the research on women/mothers and workers redesigning child welfare to suggest another conceptualisation of child welfare, one that seeks to enhance the citizenship of participants, including workers, as its fundamental aim. It is my contention that the conception of citizenship embraces both a child-centred protection and a family-centred prevention approach but adds to them. Instead of viewing either the child or the family as the unit of service, citizenship approaches encourage the involvement of other individuals and groups as worthy participants in the child welfare enterprise. They foster the development of groups where citizenship rights and responsibilities can be identified and enhanced. A comparison of these approaches - the child-centred, the family-centred and the citizenship model, in Chart 1 which is presented below.

In reporting the first phase of this research, we used the literature on empowerment to help conceptualise our work (Callahan and Lumb, 1995). However, we found it wanting. The empowerment literature is highly imprecise and includes both psychological and structural efforts under the same conceptual umbrella. It does not address the need for reciprocity, but often talks about a process where one, the worker, empowers another, the client.

Chart 1 Comparison of the Three Models of Intervention

	Child-centred prevention	Family-centred prevention	Citizenship
Focus for work	child	family	child mother father siblings reporter worker agency media
Central task	assess abuse	provide support service	enhance citizenship . economic . reciprocity . justice . participation . safety . belonging
Role of worker	assessor	enabler	participant
Theoretical base	psychosocial	ecological	structural/ feminist
Mandate	legal	organisational	community

The concept of citizenship, enhanced as it has been here with the experiences of direct participants, adds precision to the notion of empowerment. It also normalises the activities of child welfare. Rather than being punitive or patronising, the work is focused upon assisting individuals and groups to better exercise their citizenship rights and responsibilities. While we have focused upon women/mothers and workers in this research, it is clear that the same processes can apply to children, fathers, neighbours who report and so forth. Exercising citizenship is not just a responsibility of individuals and groups. Citizenship approaches to child welfare clearly focus upon the ways in which the community and state can address barriers and overcome prejudices which alienate citizens. In the process of awakening the community, estranged citizens help restore themselves.

There is a need for more conceptual work on the notion of citizenship as a theoretical umbrella for child welfare work. However, as this research has illustrated, understanding the meaning of second-class citizenship and examining how present services actually exacerbate it, is crucial to reforming child welfare.

References

Brodie, J. (1996), 'Restructuring and the New Citizenship', in I. Bakker (ed), *Rethinking Restructuring: Gender and Change in Canada*, University of Toronto Press, Toronto.

Callahan, M. and Lumb, C. (1995), 'My Cheque and my Children: The Long Road to Empowerment in Child Welfare', *Child Welfare*, LXXIV, no. 3, May/June, pp. 795-819.

Diorio, W.D. (1992), Parental Perceptions of the Authority of Public Child Welfare Caseworkers. Families in Society', *The Journal of Contemporary Human Services*, vol. 4, no. 3, pp. 55-64.

Dominelli, L. and McLeod, E. (1989), *Feminist Social Work,* Macmillan, London.

Gordon, L. (1986), 'Feminism and Social Control: The Case of Child Abuse and Neglect' in J. Mitchell. and A. Oakley (eds), *What is Feminism? a Re-examination*, Pantheon Press, New York.

Hutchison, E. (1992), 'Child Welfare as a Woman's Issue: Families in Society', in *The Journal of Contemporary Human Services*, February, pp. 67-77.

Krane, J. (1994), *The Transformation of Women into Mother Protectors: An Examination of Child Protection Practices in Cases of Child Sexual Abuse.* Unpublished doctoral dissertation, University of Toronto, School of Social Work.

Kymlicka, W. (1992), *Recent Work in Citizenship Theory*, Corporate Policy and Research, Multiculturalism and Citizenship Canada, Ottawa.

L'Huiller, E. (1994), *Neglecting Mothers: A Feminist Analysis of the Victorian Child Protection System,* Unpublished Masters thesis, University of Melbourne, Women's Studies, Department of History.

Magura, S. and Moses, B. (1984), 'Clients as Evaluators in Child Protective Services', *Child Welfare*, LXIII, no. 2, March-April, pp. 99-112.

Mason, J. (1993), *Child Welfare Policy: Critical Australian Perspectives*, Sydney: Hale and Ironmonger.

Moreau, M. and Leonard, L. (1989), *Empowerment through a Structural Approach to Social Work*, Carleton University, School of Social Work, Ottawa.

Mullender, A. and Ward, D. (1991), *Self-Directed Groupwork: Users take Action for Empowerment*, Whiting and Birch, London.

Novick, M. and Volpe, R. (1989), 'Perspectives on Social Practice', *Children at Risk Project*, The Laidlaw Foundation, Toronto.

Parton, C. and Parton, N. (1989), 'Women, the Family and Child Protection', *Critical Social Policy*, pp. 39-49.

Pelton, L. (1978), 'Child Abuse and Neglect: The Myth of Classlessness', *American Journal of Orthopsychiatry*, 48, pp. 4.

Pinker, R. (1971) *Social Theory and Social Policy*, Heinemann Educational Books, Ltd., London.

Preston-Shoot, M. (1992), 'Empowerment, Partnership and Authority in Groupwork Practice: A Training Contribution', *Groupwork*, vol. 5, no. 2, pp. 5-30.

Smith, B. and Smith, T. (1990), 'For Love and Money: Women as Foster Mothers', *Affilia*, vol. 5, no. 1, pp. 66-80.

Swift, K. (1991), 'Contradictions in Child Welfare: Neglect and Responsibility', in C. Baines, P. Evans and S. Neysmith (eds), *Women's Caring: Feminist Perspectives on Social Welfare*, McClelland and Stewart, Toronto.

Thorpe, R. (1993), 'Empowerment Groupwork with Parents of Children in Care', in J. Mason (ed), *Child Welfare Policy: Critical Australian Perspectives*, Hale and Ironmonger, Sydney.

4 A Community Approach to Urban Child Welfare in Canada

BILL LEE

Introduction

Child welfare in Canada, as in other jurisdictions, has always had to work with families and children whose troubles tend to be defined as existing primarily in the realm of the personal (Macintyre, 1993). At the same time, many social work practitioners and writers are well aware that the roots of the majority of these problems lie at a deeper social level (Wharf, 1997; Carniol, 1995; Benn, 1981). Unemployment, inadequate housing, racial discrimination and sexism, for example, all contribute to the difficulties faced by the families served by child welfare agencies. However, legislation and services are basically conceived and structured as remedial and reactive, focusing on the identification of, and service to, families who are experiencing immediate difficulty, even crisis. At the same time, the recent popularity of the slogan, 'It takes a community to raise a child', indicates that there is a growing, albeit belated and cloudy, recognition that the well-being of children depends not only on the health of the personalities of their caregivers but on the networks of social, economic and political networks in which they live[1].

Ontario is a jurisdiction which, in a general way, can be seen to have recognised this orientation since the mid-1960s. Provincial legislation directs child welfare agencies[2] to address not only conditions of 'protection' but also 'the prevention of circumstances requiring the protection of children' (Child Welfare Act of Ontario, 1965). Though prevention is alluded to, no guidelines have been provided as to how it should actually be implemented, and child welfare organisations have been left to themselves to decide whether services would be mounted and if they were, what these would be. For a number of authors (Wharf, 1979; Barr and McLaughlin, 1975; Barr, 1973), prevention in child welfare is equated with community work.

While there may be other ways to look at the notion, for example, early identification and intervention, this paper focuses on a community approach which entails intervention in and with the networks and institutions that constitute the web of relationships in which families and children live. It must be said that relatively few Ontario child welfare agencies have utilised this methodology to any great degree. Some have mounted community programmes only to cut them as successive governments have reduced funding in all areas of child welfare.

The Children's Aid Society of Metropolitan Toronto (CASMT), however, seemed to accept the position of the authors mentioned above and was perhaps the first one to mount a community work programme in the child welfare arena (Oswin, 1984). To its credit, it has persevered with various levels of effort and through cycles of more or less adequate resources. While some references will be made to other programmes in the province of Ontario, it is primarily the community work approach of the CASMT that will be considered in this chapter.

The purpose of this chapter is to examine the use of a community work approach in attempting to improve the lives of children and families. In Ontario, as in most jurisdictions in North America, this approach is a somewhat novel one. Thus, it is useful to try to come to an understanding of how a somewhat marginal social work approach (Wharf, 1997) that seeks to assist families by ameliorating surrounding conditions rather than through casework with children and families has developed and been able to survive under a variety of hostile conditions.

The chapter will not evaluate the outcomes of the CASMT programme. Rather, it will take an historical approach, describing the beginnings of the programme, its development, its struggles and its current situation. The conclusion of the chapter is based in part, on discussions held with the present community workers. The purpose is not only to bring a contemporary voice into the work, but also to assist in the reflection on the meaning of the longevity of a programme that, as already noted, is unique or marginal in terms of approaches to child welfare in Canada.

Locating the Author

Feminists (Bishop , 1994; Adamson, Briskin and McPhail, 1987) and other structurally oriented practitioners (Lakey, 1987) have pointed out the importance of locating oneself in relation to the issues that are being discussed. There are a number of 'locations' that are probably significant in the writing of this paper. The first is that it is being written by someone who is committed to community work as an important form of social work practice. I believe that community practice can be seen as having the potential to act constructively in dealing with a tension in social work - private troubles versus public issues.

A second 'location' comes from my early work in child welfare, as a caseworker. The experience of working with families in crisis, often brought on by forces or conditions far from their making, forced me to look for larger explanations and eventually into becoming involved in community development and social action activities. I have now worked in and taught community work for almost thirty years.

Finally, in the early-1970s, I helped develop some community-based initiatives at the Catholic Children's Aid Society of Metropolitan Toronto. Also, in the mid-1970s, I worked for two years with the community work programme at the Children's Aid Society of Metropolitan Toronto. This provides the major practical context for this paper.

Specifying Community and a Community Work Approach

I will first turn to examine what is meant by the terms 'community' and 'community practice'. The word 'community' has a myriad number of definitions (Brager, Specht and Torczyner, 1987; Warren, 1983). But, it can be seen as the arena that stands at the interface between individual and family or personal life, and the larger arenas of institutional life or the economy and the state (Wharf, 1997). Community, through the networks of personal and institutional relationships, mediates the impact of the larger spheres on the personal lives of individuals and families. It is also a place where personal networks and discourses begin to engage the larger institutional arenas. Community, is thus made up and partakes of both personal and institutional life. Community has also two foundations: (a) among a group of people who live in a given geographic area, and; (b) among a group of people sharing some important attribute or function (Plant, 1974). These orientations to community are not mutually exclusive. One can share a common trait like 'race' or class with others and also live in the same neighbourhood. For the most part, in this paper however, the term 'community' will be utilised in its geographic sense.

Community Practice and Empowerment

There are also a variety of ways in which we try to come to understand community work practice. Some authors see it as planning and co-ordinating social services to be more efficient and effective (Murphy, 1954). Others see it as a means to redress power imbalance in society (Kahn, 1982; Rubin and Rubin, 1986). Still others see it as a means whereby community members more effectively share limited resources to create a better life (McKnight, 1996; Ross, 1967; Biddle and Biddle, 1965). Rothman and Tropman (1987) have articulated perhaps the most well known approach, one that places these models in a coherent framework, social action, the alteration of power relationships, locality development, the identification and mobilisation of community capacity and social planning, the improvement in the level and quality of services. As will be seen, the orientation to community practice in child welfare has involved primarily, though not exclusively the second of the Rothman and Tropman models - locality development. The emphasis has been on the recognition of the ability of people to contribute their understandings and experience to the services that effect them, and on building community capacity and the sense that they can actually influence conditions in which they live their daily lives. This latter notion, the belief or sense of efficacy in changing their circumstances comprises the notion of empowerment or to use Freire's (1970) language, a sense in people that they are subjects of the world rather than its objects.

Empowerment

Empowerment, while seen as a central goal for community work (Lee, 1992; Russel-Erlich and Rivera, 1986) is a complex and often confusing notion. It is something that must be examined critically and relative to its rootedness in the concrete experience of people. It has to be actualised through the achievement of specific objectives. In this sense, empowerment is something that informs objectives and tasks and is, in turn, informed by them. The goal of empowerment, the feeling in people that they can influence their environment, is an intimate part of community work objectives and the objectives are essential parts of empowerment. It is reflected and experienced in the actual achieving of objectives. In other words, the achievement of any of the objectives can be empowering. Further, empowerment cannot exist outside of the striving. That is, as we begin to strive for the accomplishment of one or more of the objectives - as we find that we can participate in a discussion or that by making our voices heard we begin to be listened to - we are developing a sense that we have the ability to influence our lives. Community work, at its best then, becomes 'an empowering process', the aim of which is to see people gain a greater sense of their ability to affect their environment. We are able to reflect on the utility of community development efforts by examining the extent to which there is evidence that any of the objectives that are present are met.

The way I will actually examine the community approach to practice in child welfare will be to articulate six major objectives that community workers can attempt to achieve and which are crucial elements in healthy or empowered community life. These objectives are: citizen participation, organisation development, concrete benefit, community sense, social learning and social justice. While these have been described elsewhere (Lee, 1992), I will briefly go over the objectives before utilising them in the discussion of a community approach in child welfare.

Citizen Involvement or Participation

The objective of citizen participation refers to community members making decisions, and acting on them, to try and do something about problems that are important to them, 'to help others while being helped themselves' (Rice, 1990, p. 9). Another way of saying this might be engagement in a change process or citizens actually acting on their own behalf to bring about some positive alteration in their environment. To act, however, people must see themselves as citizens, with rights, abilities and

68

the responsibility to express opinions and act to acquire the resources they need. The link to empowerment is fairly obvious. For a group of people to feel positive about their ability to influence their lives, they must actually take action. If they do not act, they will not achieve their objectives. Indeed, they might lose the sense that they can act. Participation or action can be expressed in a wide variety of ways - voting, coming to meetings, joining self-help, advocacy or social action groups, for example. If people take up leadership responsibilities in community organisations, their participation is deepened. The point of participation, however, is not simply action and leadership. It is also an expression of citizenship (Saul, 1997). Taking action as citizens has an effect on how people see themselves and how others see them or the issues for which they advocate. Problems are often ignored when citizens are not active in bringing them to public notice.

Organisation Development

Organisation development refers to the building of a new organisation or the improvement of an already existing one, by for example, gaining resources, increasing participation. A key element of power in our society is having numbers of people on our side (Moyer, 1990). Many writers (Rubin and Rubin, 1984; Alinsky, 1971) however, point out that numbers only lead to power when they are organised. An organised group in a community can stimulate energy in the form of cohesion. A people with organisation can share information on the problems they face, resources or their own skills. In short, a community organisation is important for the marshalling of effort and resources over time. Both of these endeavours are crucial in the developmental process.

Concrete Benefit or Resources

Concrete benefits refer to the achievement for the community of some specific resource, an increase in service, or the development of a new facility of some sort. These can include the creation of a community centre, obtaining an increase in government benefits or halting an event or situation which is hazardous to the population. As Thomas (1983) points out, there is a clear connection between lack of power and a people who are denied access to basic resources. As well as the utility of the actual resource, we can see a connection to empowerment. As one community worker I interviewed put it, 'People must have victories to prove to themselves that they are really capable'. It is so much easier to believe in ourselves if we are part of a successful attempt to have a particular need met. If we understand that we have achieved one thing, we can believe that we can go after others.

Sense of Community

As indicated previously, community is a term which is used with a variety of meanings (Warren, 1883; Plant, 1974). We can speak of geographically based groups like urban neighbourhoods as well as people who share common attributes like 'race' or culture. Whatever the bonding factor however, it is important for the members to have a positive sense of themselves as a specific group and a belief in the validity of their perceptions of their experience.

Additionally, people live in an alienating and alienated world dominated by technical efficiency and bureaucratic procedures (Saul, 1997; Illich, 1972). The separateness that they experience leads not only to loneliness, but also to feelings of confusion and impotence. Alienation is disempowering. Lone individuals cannot hope to influence the powerful systems that exist all around them. Indeed, they may feel that these can act on them in the most oppressive ways. Citizenship involves the experience of connection with others (Saul, 1997). The rediscovery and re-establishment of a sense of community - a common experience, common dreams - is an important contributor to a sense of influence and is a necessary component in any struggle to achieve social change.

Social Learning

Skills learning refers to the processes whereby people in the community acquire new skills. To know that they have the ability to accomplish something, that they are not simply wishing that they could do it, is a crucial determinant of their self-image. Their feelings of self-esteem are often influenced by the realisation that they have learned how to do something - chair a meeting, write a news release, research some information, or deal with a bureaucracy or handle a complex situation. Community workers spend considerable energy assisting activists to learn how to operate their own organisation or helping them to develop strategies to influence power holders (Rubin and Rubin, 1986; Alinsky, 1971).

Secondly, social learning refers to community members developing a useful analysis of themselves, their community, the larger society and/or the problems with which they are faced. As the Women's Movement has demonstrated, to have an understanding of the social, political and economic factors that shape the conditions of their lives can help to free them from self-blame and debilitating guilt for their inability to be as successful as they would wish (Adamson et al, 1989). To develop an active and healthy community, people must have the opportunities and means to learn.

Social learning is crucial for people to continue the struggle of development. If they do not develop a critical analysis in solidarity with the other people with whom they work - of what they are doing, attempting to achieve, and the environment in which they are striving to do it, they will tend to develop very naive strategies that will lead to defeat, disillusionment or co-optation.

Social Justice

Social justice addresses the notion of the wider and deeper structural issues of inequality. While community work generally tends to focus on issues of a local or community specific nature, practitioners are aware of the broader social and political context (Lakey et al, 1995; Bishop, 1994; Adamson et al, 1989). Issues of rights and fairness, underfunded services, inadequate housing, sex discrimination and racism, for example, lie at the heart of many of the issues that disadvantage communities. While these have local expressions, they are not simply local. Community workers become involved in larger movements and coalitions to deal with these types of social justice issues. They assist the people and organisations with whom they work to do the same.

Interrelationships among Objectives

While I consider each of these objectives individually, it is important to be clear that they are not discrete but interrelated (See Figure 1). For example, participation can be linked to the attainment of a concrete benefit or the development of an organisation. A viable organisation, as noted earlier, is necessary to draw the members of a community into a coherent force for the attainment of benefits. Learning the workings of an organisation as well as those of the social, political and economic environment, is required to make the organisation successful. A positive sense of community identity can result from the successful work of its 'own' organisation. At the same time the development of a positive sense of identity and connections among people should shape the nature of the organisation and provide a vision for their work.

It is also important to be clear that practically speaking, community work projects do not, and cannot, focus on all these objectives all of the time. Resources, time available and local conditions shape what objectives can be pursued at any one point. However, the deliberately exclusive pursuit of a single objective might not be reflective of a solid community work process. For example, the development of a sound and efficient organisation without reference to the objectives of community sense or citizen participation can lead to inappropriate services, unnecessary internal conflict, elitism and alienation of those not involved with the leadership of such an organisation. The temptation to formalise or professionalise an organisation can also alienate the community that it was set up to serve (Cain 1993). Focusing solely on the acquisition of a concrete benefit can lead to co-optation where people are 'bought off' and led to believe that they no longer need to struggle (Piven and Cloward, 1979). Furthermore, if they are only interested in one issue, a failure to achieve it may sap energy from carrying on with others.

Thus, community work is a complex business that requires considerable thought and discipline. It is important to be clear what objectives the community needs to achieve at a particular time but also important to understand where it is in terms of the range of objectives being pursued.

Figure 1   **Interrelationships among Community Development Objectives**

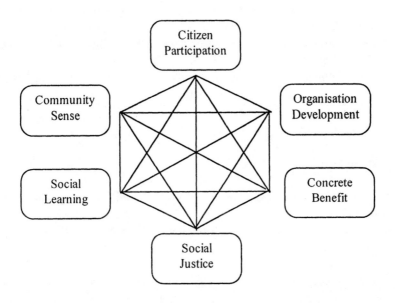

Community Work in CASMT
The City and the Children's Aid Society

Metropolitan Toronto is a city of over three and a half million people, the largest urban centre in Canada. It is situated in the industrial heartland of the country and until fairly recently, was understood to be its most economically comfortable area. Since the mid-1950s the city has grown considerably, not only in size but in complexity. There have been successive waves of migration which over time have profoundly altered the racial and ethnic makeup of the city. There have been significant groups from Western Europe, then Eastern Europe, the Caribbean, Latin America and most recently Africa and Asia. It also is home to the largest population of Native or First Nations people in the country, a group who within themselves represent a rich range of experiences and cultures. Thus, it has developed from an almost exclusively European peoples to an extremely diverse mix of 'races' and cultures and is thought of, at least by its inhabitants, as one of the most cosmopolitan urban areas in the world. The Children's Aid Society of Metropolitan Toronto (CASMT) was established in 1891. With a current budget of sixty-two million dollars and over six hundred employees, it serves approximately 7,350 families covering 19,000 children and youths[3]. It is one of the largest child welfare agencies in North America. As indicated, it offers a broad variety of services, most of them focused on the welfare of children.

Early Days - Beginning with Social Planning

While the Child Welfare Act of 1965 gave some credibility to the idea of community approaches, child welfare agencies in Ontario had often been engaged in efforts aimed at improving social planning and the co-ordination of social services (Barr, 1979). The complexity of offering social services in a quickly growing and complex urban area like Metropolitan (Metro) Toronto demanded that social agencies work together, at least periodically. For example, in 1964-5, the Catholic Children's Aid Society and CASMT were involved in joint service planning with a local settlement house and other service agencies for an urban renewal project. However, it was not until after the 1965 Child Welfare Act that any efforts were directed to actually working with grassroots community groups and organisations. In 1968-69, the CASMT became a partner with the Family Service Association in developing a joint service strategy to a few geographic communities.

It should be stated that other agencies in Ontario were experimenting with community approaches. For example, the York Region CAS, located just to the north of Metropolitan Toronto, had a community work programme from 1972 to the mid-1980s. In the early-1970s, there was some work done by the Catholic Children's Aid Society of Metro Toronto with the city's First Nations community organisations primarily to improve or make more culturally appropriate services available to Native children in care (Beamish and Lee, 1969). Later in the 1970s, the same agency developed a community work programme that lasted until the mid-1990s.

Decentralisation and Participation

The CASMT began deploying child protection workers into so-called 'high risk' communities on a part-time basis in 1968. While initially these workers were simply seen as providing a kind of adjunct service to caseworkers (Cross Branch Community Workers Group, 1980), the approach evolved into one that reflected a developmental community work orientation. The definition that was reportedly used (Oswin 1980, pp. 58-59) identifies community work as:

> working within a child welfare context, to enable low income communities to identify their own needs, as well as identifying larger social problems and liaising with other interested community groups to facilitate social change.

There is an obvious emphasis on process, assisting with needs identification and networking with like minded groups. We can sense that social justice - the facilitation of social change - was to be an important objective, though in a somewhat abstract sense.

Clearly, whatever the definition, a major objective at the beginning was to address citizen participation. The concern was to allow and encourage community involvement in the service delivery of the agency. Beginning in June 1968, a committee of social workers and residents of Regent Park in Toronto where the first major public housing project in Canada developed[4], began to meet to consider issues of the quality and appropriateness of child welfare service delivery to the people living there. These meetings continued into the fall of 1970, when the Regent Park Services Unit opened. Child protection services were delivered out of this office in conjunction with other social services and with input of community residents (Barr, 1979). This marked the first occasion when residents were seriously involved in the design of child welfare services to their community.

Part of impetus for this development was rooted in the demands of local communities themselves for input into the kinds of services they were being given (Oswin, 1980). At the same time, it probably also reflected a generally heightened consciousness that political leaders were fallible and social institutions were often seriously flawed (Newbury, 1989).

Moreover, 'people were no longer willing to passively assent to accept everything they were told' (Cross Branch Community Work Group, 1980). It was also a reflection of relatively secure economic times and a more flexible orientation in government funding (Cross Branch Community Work Group, 1980) - at least by the standards of today.

Programme Growth and Innovative Administration

The numbers of workers grew from three part timers who spent two-fifths of their time doing community work and the remainder traditional casework in the early-1970s, to ten full timers by the early-1980s.

During this period an interesting administrative structure emerged for the programme. The CASMT was (and is) organised by branches. That is, while the operation of the organisation had a strong central management and service component, finance, liaison with child treatment institutions, court services, planning, staff training, and many of the services particularly involved in direct work with children and families in the community were, and are, delivered from branch offices serving large geographic districts[5].

Each part of the metropolitan area had a geographically based branch office which provided a range of child protection services. The community workers were employed and administered by these branch offices. As the programme gradually grew and matured, a need was identified for specific community work consultation for the workers. With rare exceptions, branch managers had been trained and had experience only with individual and family social work practice. As part of their innovative approach, rather than centralise the operation under one supervisor, a collective structure was developed whereby community workers gathered bi-weekly in a 'cross-branch' group to provide support for each other. The structure subsequently developed roughly as is indicated in Figure 2 below.

Figure 2   Organisation of the Community Worker Programme in CASMT

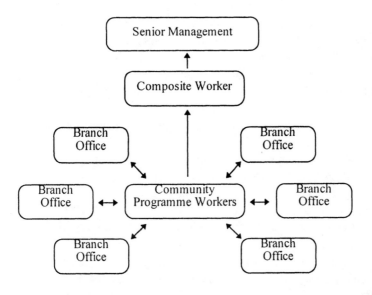

Initially, the group acted as a simple consultative, information-sharing and support body to its members. Decision-making involving project choices, priorities and similar activities remained with the branch office. By 1975, when the compliment of workers stood at seven, the workers 'identified the need for improved consultation and programme development' (Oswin, 1984, p. 43). Discussions were held with senior management and, in 1976, a rather unique organisational structure emerged. While decisions about project choice and priorities would remain with the branch administrations, three functions were identified which would be taken on by the cross branch group itself. These were: chairing the group, which included general programme administration like scheduling and chairing meetings and most importantly, negotiating with senior management on behalf of the programme; handling training which included liaison with the agency training department; and, addressing social issues which involved staffing the Social Issues Committee of the agency Board of Directors. The novel approach to administering these functions was to mandate a collective leadership to take responsibility for co-ordinating the overall programme. It was referred to as a 'composite worker'[6]. The 'composite worker' position involved time from three workers which added to a total of one full-time post. The time and tasks allocated to the 'composite worker' were: two days per week for the chairperson; two days per week for training; and, one day per week for working on social issues (Oswin, 1984, p. 44).

This was the only programme in the agency that worked without a direct service manager. It was also the only programme where line social workers dealt in a direct manner with senior administration (see Figure 2), without having to work through the layers of organisational bureaucracy. Also, as far as community workers were concerned, this structuring of their working relations mirrored the collective, non-hierarchical organisational relationships they wished to see fostered within their communities.

During this period, the major focus of community work developed into one of assisting communities toward self-sufficiency by helping them to apply for funds, usually from provincial government programmes and ministries and organising community-based services. Allied to this approach was the work of identifying and grooming leadership personnel who could engage state and voluntary agencies in considerations of service quality and secure appropriate funding for the community-based organisations.

Community Resource Development

Another important development in the agency's community approach was reflected in the nature of the objectives that the community workers were seeking in the mid-to-late-1970s. As indicated above, earlier efforts were aimed at consulting with grassroots groups and decentralising services. This was seen as allowing the community to reshape the type of the services that the CASMT was delivering, a participation objective. The emphasis evolved to one focused on the development of local resources (Cross Branch Community Work Group, 1980) which would render the community more self-sufficient. For example, one worker from the North Branch was instrumental in the development of a child and family centre that served the needs of low-income families, primarily led by single women. This appears to have been fairly typical work for the community workers. At least two other workers were endeavouring to assist community organisations to acquire resources to mount locally based and run social and recreational services. Thus, workers and the programme were strongly focused on assisting their communities in developing organisations and gaining concrete benefits, aiming their work at increasing the amount and quality of the infrastructure.

Engaging Social Justice Issues

Interestingly, as Ontario in the late-1970s was seeing cutbacks to social services in general and to child welfare in particular, the CASMT community work programme actually expanded for a time. This expansion involved not only an increase in the worker compliment to ten, but also in the vision for the operation of the programme. While the definition of community work had included the notion of social change, actual practice had been rooted in local communities and local issues. That is, whatever the root or systemic causality of problems, it was the local expression of these issues that CASMT community workers helped community members address. In 1980, a branch report (Cross Branch Community Work Group, 1980) made a case that there was need for the programme to deal with more than improvement in local conditions, that larger considerations were also important. The strongly structurally-oriented flavour of the concerns is caught in the following statement from the report:

> It can no longer be only a question of providing services to enhance the quality of life when many of the pre-conditions for survival are being systematically weakened through cutbacks, freezes and increasing public antipathy towards people who are perceived as 'free loaders'. The Cross Branch Community Work Group is proposing that future community work activity be structured to allow a co-ordinated approach to common issues simultaneously, at both the local and Metro levels. This approach would focus on those problems which are threatening to cripple the very ability of families to survive: housing, day care, illiteracy, levels of social assistance, immigration policies.

After lengthy discussions with senior management, the response was a direction by management in 1981, that a small amount of community work time be allocated to working on the issues of housing and day care

79

(Oswin, 1984, p. 47), two important concerns in child welfare. The focus on structural issues expanded in 1982, when some of the programme resources were provided to a group, the Sole Support Parents Coalition, contesting changes to provincial regulations which would have significantly reduced benefits to single parent families.

As suggested above, it is interesting that this addition of a structural element to the agenda of the community work programme should come about when it did. At this time, the economy in Canada had slowed down, inflation was relatively high, and there was a growing retreat from the activism of the previous decade. Governments were cutting back and community work programmes were suffering everywhere. Sometimes, the programme came under attack from local politicians who felt threatened by some of the initiatives or groups supported by workers from the programme. How then was this alteration managed?

Oswin (1984) suggests that not only this expansion but most of the subsequent developments, including the inception of the programme, came about through the initiative of the workers themselves. This argument has merit. The document, *Framework For The 80s* (Cross Branch Community Workers Group, 1980), identifying the programme's future development, was well-researched and thought out. At the same time, while workers can advocate for particular services, this does not necessarily result in their realisation. What would account for the effectiveness of the community workers' lobbying for their own programme?

Two factors might have contributed to the effectiveness of the group in this case. First, there was the connection with various communities enjoyed by the community worker programme. Unlike individual caseworkers, these workers had relatively high and positive profiles in the communities within which they worked. The relationships which they had cultivated over the years had not only provided the agency with some positive public relations, but they had also recruited strong external advocates for the community work programme. At times when agency administration looked to save money by cutting the funding of the programme, allies could be, and were, mobilised to publicly advocate for the workers.

The second factor that may have played a part in this success was the unique manner in which the programme was structured. The regular cross branch meetings and the existence of an elected composite worker management system may have provided the programme with three advantages. First, meeting regularly together and electing their own administration tended to provide a strong sense of cohesion. Moreover, as the programme only 'belonged' to any one branch in bits and pieces, this may have reduced the likelihood of a coherent opposition to it throughout the agency. Indeed, it may have resulted in some widely dispersed internal support. Thus, there was a kind of dispersed accountability that perhaps made the programme a difficult one around which an opposition could effectively be gathered. Finally, because of the way the programme was administratively structured, the community workers had more direct access to senior management than any other programme in the agency. They did not have to go through supervisors and up the lines to senior management. This meant that their messages would be unencumbered by the various institutional and bureaucratic imperatives that those of a more typical programme would have had to carry. In sum, the community worker programme had a strong identity; more autonomy and access to decision-making than one would expect within a bureaucratic environment; and, external advocates. This meant that they were able to act for themselves to protect their programme, at least for a time.

Programme Cuts

While the programme was able to protect itself solidly for a while, it could not maintain this position indefinitely. Late in 1982, the Society was confronted by a significant budget cut from the Province and the programme, while again mobilising significant community support, had lost three positions by the middle of the following year (Oswin, 1984). Later, in 1984, another position was lost, bringing the compliment down to six workers.

Continuing Resource Development

While the internal wrangling went on, the major community work focus continued to be resource development. A number of parent and child centres, administered and staffed by local residents and volunteers and supported by agency community workers, came into being. Efforts also went into developing and working with groups that focused on housing advocacy programmes and local legal services. There was a considerable interest on the part of the provincial government in both these areas and a certain amount of money was available during this period.

During the 1980s, the programme became increasingly involved with what was termed 'ethno-specific' communities (Cross Branch Community Workers, 1990). Throughout the 1960s and particularly the 1970s Toronto had seen a large influx of immigrants from the Caribbean, particularly Jamaica. Also, during the 1970s, the city had increasingly become a destination of choice for a wide variety of immigrants and refugees. These hailed primarily from countries in Latin America and South East Asia and constituted groups that had not previously been represented in any significant numbers.

Not surprisingly, settlement and translation programmes were the principle needs identified at this time. To meet these needs, some monies became available through federal programmes. Community workers became involved in communities assisting local groups to develop proposals, build their organisations and plan programmes. They also became involved in identifying the need for various social agency personal to be prepared for dealing with people of non-English-speaking cultures and developing training appropriate for meeting this purpose.

The major roles for the CASMT community workers at this time were: identifying funding sources, fund-raising; and assisting in the development of organisational skills. There was also a good deal of activity in the areas of programme development. The experience was that while people who lived in disadvantaged communities were well able to express their experience and needs, for the development of effective programme responses, specific assistance was required in organising the effort.

While it is not clear that the participation objective was being ignored, it is obvious that organisation development, concrete benefits and social learning objectives were the ones highlighted here.

Continuing Engagement in Social Justice Issues

During the latter years of the 1980s, there was a continued commitment to local service organisation development and a growing interest in directly addressing social justice objectives in a larger arena. As globalisation and the free movement of capital took increasing hold (Rifkin, 1995), the economic position of the country became worse. Unemployment and poverty levels rose in Canada (McQuaig, 1995). A variety of anti-poverty groups grew up. Some of these were locally based while others had a cross-city focus. CASMT community work time was allotted to a variety of these endeavours.

Child poverty in a country as wealthy as Canada and a city as rich as Toronto had become a significant public issue and one worker became involved in Action 2000. This was a coalition of groups centred in Toronto. It focused on maintaining the public profile of the issue and eliminating child poverty by the year 2000 and espoused aims which endorsed those contained in the United Nation's Convention on the Rights of the Child.

While non-profit housing was at the time still receiving some funding, the settlement of large numbers of refugees and immigrants from both inside and outside the country, was leading to a serious shortage of reasonably priced and adequate housing. Some community worker time went to a network of agencies working on shelters, particularly for youth. Another of the community workers worked with a group aimed at influencing housing policy. Reflecting a concern with racial issues, the same worker sat on another group aimed at ensuring the rights of equal access to adequate housing (Cross Branch Community Worker's Group, 1990) for different ethnic/racial groups.

Given the limited resources of the programme, and keeping in mind that what is presented above is a very sketchy and incomplete identification of the range of involvements undertaken during the period, the work of the community work programme is remarkable. It suggests not only a commitment by the programme personal but also a commitment of the agency as a whole to a wider understanding of child welfare services.

The Contemporary Situation

At present the community work programme has been maintained at a level of six full-time workers and a half-time supervisor who reports to the manager for the Centre of Clinical Research and Prevention Services. The alteration in the administration of the programme, that is, its integration into the regular bureaucratic model, came about in 1994, as part of a reorganisation of the agency. The programme, while continuing to be based in the branches as a means of connecting with all sectors of the city, became part of a larger prevention department that is administered out of the central office. In more recent years, there have been no attempts to downsize the programme. This is owed in part to the acquisition of some funding from the Children's Aid Foundation[7] as well as the credibility that the programme has developed within the agency (Community Work Group, 1998).

Increasing Complexity

The workers in the programme continue to work in the area of local community resource creation. Two workers are involved in the formation of local economic development projects. Given the economic downturn and lack of employment opportunities for so many low-income families, this is a not unsurprising involvement. Another continues to work with residents of a public housing project in a western section of the city to develop programmes to deal with child safety and family support. At the same time, the trend that developed in the late-1980s and early-1990s to focus on wider social issues appears to have increased. Workers have noted (Community Worker Group Discussion, 1998) that while residents are still very concerned about local conditions and responding to specific community needs, the rightist shift of governments had encouraged, even necessitated, people looking at root problems that demanded a wider mobilisation. Four issues were identified that had become major foci for community work: lack of appropriate child care; child poverty; inadequate levels of public welfare and housing. Interestingly, with the exception of the public welfare issue[8], these are the same items that were identified earlier. The difference is that these problems have become more generally recognised. The result has been that all the workers are more involved in assisting community groups to join coalitions. Additionally, the workers find themselves more directly involved in these coalitions.

An important factor that has been identified here is that change, often complex and regressive, has been occurring so quickly that there has not been time to work with community members in supportive and educative ways. For example, workers have found themselves required to become spokespersons for groups at some points. They have taken on advocacy functions. This has led to some struggles around the community work role which is aimed at facilitating the development of community competence. In its framework for action, the community workers group has identified the following as an overall goal for its work (Prevention Team, 1997):

> enabling the collective actions of diverse community members to support children, youth and families by building on individual and community capacities.

The members of the group are having to wrestle with both issues of utility which raise questions about their effectiveness as advocates alongside those of adherence to community work values and the extent to which they are adequately addressing the communities' needs and ability to develop themselves. A significant community social work principle is that the people should be in control of what is going on (Kelleher and Whelan, 1992). Can the current situation be managed in a way that deals with the concrete and immediate needs for sophisticated responses and actions while at the same time engaging community members in meaningful ways so that they gain in knowledge and experience and develop confidence amongst community groups?

Another factor that has also increased the complexity of the community work task is one that is referred to as the 'isms' (Community Worker Group, 1998). Canadian communities, particularly in Toronto, have become increasingly diverse (Lee et al, 1996) and issues of 'race', gender and culture are seen as in many parts of the industrialised world underlying or being involved in almost all issues (Dominelli, 1988). One response of the Community Work Programme has been involvement in the Achieving Collaboration Group, a city wide collective of community workers, residents, leaders and activists. As well as networking and information sharing, the focus of this group has been to develop a sophisticated analysis of the social and political realities that Toronto communities are facing and to formulate educational strategies in response. While all the 'isms' are raised in this vein, the issues of 'race' and culture have been perhaps the most predominant (Community Worker Group Discussion, 1998). The importance of assisting various diverse communities to find and express their legitimate voice is recognised by the community workers. At the same time, as indicated earlier, they are being required to respond swiftly to complicated issues such as changing regulations to welfare and cuts in funding to a tremendous number of community-based and state-run social welfare institutions. This raises a third issue with which they must deal - a reduced community resource base.

In the previous two decades community-based groups and outreach programmes of state agencies were either in a state of expansion or at least were relatively stable. Cuts started to appear in the late-1980s, but in the last six years and particularly the last two, the process has accelerated and the number of these agencies and programmes has been drastically reduced as governments cut back funding. In a situation of high unemployment and flattening wage levels, non-profit sector groups like the United Way scramble to simply maintain funding levels.

As a result of the shifting economic climate, the range of community-based agencies with which the CASMT programme co-operates has shrunk considerably from its earlier levels. For example, almost all housing advocacy funding has been cancelled and most social planning organisations in Ontario have seen significant cutbacks in their financing. These have been so severe that some local organisations have had to go out of business. Often, a CASMT community worker may find herself as the lone worker in an area where needs and demands have increased substantially.

These changes have, therefore, impacted on the working conditions of the practitioners. Workers feel caught in the dilemma of choosing among competing demands. The legitimate need to respond to a crisis of wide ranging importance such as a twenty percent cutback in welfare rates, for example, often conflicts with the equally legitimate but longer-term need to work on the development of the organisation or leadership potential and education. There are no simple answers here. Moreover, such rapid and unsupported change can demoralise workers if they lack support networks and links with other professionals.

Clarifying Objectives

To try to come to grips with the dilemmas posed in the present harsh economic climate, the community work team has sought to rethink its strategy and worked to draft a series of objectives to bring some sense of coherence to dealing with the issues that they are facing. The penultimate document lists seven of them. The outcomes of their considerations are reproduced in Figure 3 below.

Some interesting connections with the model put forward earlier in the chapter are now becoming apparent. It is clear, by the attention given to the array of objectives, that the programme is attempting to take a broad developmental approach to its community practice. With the exception of concrete benefits, each of the important objectives in community development is mentioned. Thus, they have sought to straddle the divide between structural forces which are impinging on their day-to-day work whilst at the same time seeking to motivate the community they are working with to take collective action which serves its own concerns and responds more appropriately to their needs as they define them.

Interestingly, the workers have indicated that they are in many cases still involved with local resource development as in the economic development initiatives, for example. Again, this reflects the difficulty that community workers would have were they to focus solely on either the structural or personal dimensions of change. Thinking globally and acting locally retains its appeal. The final draft of their document may well reflect that commitment. At the same time, while clarity is important, the complexity and rapidity of change is making it difficult for the programme to achieve a productive balance between these two forces.

Figure 3   Community Work Programme and Community Work Model Objectives

Community Work Programme Objectives	Community Work Model Objectives
1. To increase residents' participation in decisions that will shape the community.	Community Sense
2. To increase individual and community self-esteem.	Community Sense
3. To increase participation of residents in community identified and directed actions designed to enhance child and youth well-being and reduce the incidence of child neglect and abuse.	Citizen Participation
4. To increase the identification and utilisation of individual capacities that contribute to a community building process supportive of children, youth and families.	Organisation Development (Leadership)
5. To increase the availability of information, both within the community and the agency, related to the social, political and economic inequalities that place children at risk.	Social Learning (Social/Political Analysis)
6. To increase the links between local, Metro, provincial and federal social justice activities.	Social Justice
7. To increase the participation of branch and agency staff in CASMT Community Work Programme Activities.	N/A

Conclusion

The community work approach at CASMT is about thirty years old. This is a significant achievement for a programme that, as previously noted while innovative, represents a marginal methodology within social work. It appears now that it occupies a relatively secure place in the organisation and is able to focus some effort on developing itself around a solid array of objectives.

There are a number of challenges it will face in accomplishing this task, but two predominate in relation to those faced by other workers in child welfare. The first is how to address the mandate to focus on the development of community capacity or self-sufficiency. As indicated earlier in the chapter, this requires attention being given to a variety of objectives and arriving at some sort of balance in going after them. This is a major issue that currently occupies an important place in the thinking of the group because of the complexity of the environment and the relatively thin resources available.

A second issue that the programme is facing, is the place of advocacy in the community approach. On the one hand, it is clear that the programme provides groups with important skills, particularly of leadership and status, not immediately available from the ranks of most groups of disadvantaged people. The speed of change and the complexity of issues is legitimately seen as rendering many grassroots groups confused and vulnerable[9]. There is clearly a need here to which workers have responded at various times. At the same time, there is unquestionable recognition that a strong advocacy role, while filling the need for quick and intelligent responses, may not contribute much to long-term community capacity building. The dilemma is how to balance the need for advocacy with that of more developmental work.

These two challenges appear to lie at the heart of what the approach is about and calls up an analogy with the struggle faced by caseworkers. The crises encountered by families tend to require immediate and focused intervention on the part of the worker. At the same time the worker, by instinct and training, wishes to provide a supportive developmental service to the families that will allow them to handle a crisis themselves. Both the caseworker and community worker have complex objectives that they know must be dealt with in a co-ordinated manner. Both bring skills, status and power that allow them to act on behalf of their clientele. Both also wrestle with doing their jobs with a lack of adequate resources. The demands of both jobs are extreme. However, the community workers have a unique factor at their disposal - their primary mandate as a preventative service. This raises the question of whether emphasising an advocacy role is consistent with the pursuit of the objective of developing capacity or self-sufficiency in communities so that they can manage their own affairs.

Workers can and do question each other on the utility of responding to crises as advocates. As mentioned above, this programme is thirty years old and is certainly no longer experimental. The workers have gained experience and a structural perspective that is driving them to confront very fundamental practice concerns. What are the legitimate concrete objectives that can reasonably be addressed? Can any community-oriented child welfare approach, particularly in the prevailing environment, undertake services that can be fundamentally preventative or developmental? How do we balance prevention and development work with the need to respond to crisis?

These are difficult questions and they are obviously not the sole responsibility of this programme to answer. Indeed, without too much alteration in language, they could probably relate to any number of child welfare and social work approaches in a variety of situations. Nevertheless, they are particularly important to this programme with its complex mix of mandate, expertise and experience and the attempt to address them indicates a maturity and confidence that will be required in meeting the challenges of working within the very complex social realities of the future.

Notes

1   Thanks are due to Sharon Richards (Supervisor) Joan Davis (Manager of the Centre for the Clinical Research and Prevention Services) Valerie Hartling, Ken Sosa, Anne, Fitzpatrick Cindy Hemelstein and Colin Hughes. One worker was on leave.
2   In Ontario, child welfare agencies are mandated and funded by the provincial government. At the same time, they are administered by local boards of directors who identify what they see as local issues for service and prioritise them in terms of the provision of service.

3   This does not include services like adoption, adoption disclosure and the provision of information to ex-Crown wards.

4   Completed in the mid-1950s and hailed as a progressive and humane approach to dealing with housing for disadvantaged people, by the mid-1960s it was recognised as one of the most troubled communities in the city.

5   Until 1 January 1998, the area of the municipality of Metropolitan Toronto was made up of five smaller cities and one borough. The branch boundaries more or less conformed to those of cities and boroughs. These entities have been amalgamated into one city. The branches' boundaries have not been altered.

6   Interestingly, the composite positions were not filled by appointment by management but through election among the community workers themselves.I vividly remember attending a very energetic meeting in 1978, when large numbers of community members from across the city jammed a hall to demand from the CASMT Board of Directors that the programme's services be maintained in their communities. They were successful.The election of a rigid right wing government in 1996 has led to the cancelling of almost all assisted housing programmes in Ontario.

7   This foundation is allied with the Children's Aid Society but is a separate private non-profit organisation which funds a variety of projects that address the needs of children.

8   One of the first actions that the right wing Tory government undertook on taking office was to cut welfare benefits by twenty per cent.

9   It is believed by many that the present Tory government is deliberately copying the New Zealand strategy of attempting to dismantle the welfare state by making wide ranging and extremely quick changes in a number of policy areas including welfare, health care, workers' rights and education. This has made it difficult for community groups to mount coherent opposition.

References

Adamson, N., Briskin, L. and McPhail, M. (1989), *Feminist Organising for Change,* Oxford University Press, Toronto.

Alinsky, S. (1971), *Rules for Radicals,* Vintage Press, New York.

Barr, D. (1979), 'The Regent Park Community Service Unit: Partnership can Work', in B. Wharf (ed), *Community Work in Canada,* McClelland and Stewart, Toronto, pp. 27-50.

Barr, D. (1971), 'Doing Prevention', *Ontario Association of Children's Aid Society Journal,* February, pp. 8-13.

Barr, D. and McLaughlin, A. (1975), 'A Community Worker Prevention Programme', *Ontario Association of Children's Aid Society Journal,* April.

Beamish, C and Lee, B. (1973), 'Catholic Children's Aid Society (CCAS) and Native People', *Ontario Association of Children's Aid Society Journal,* January, pp. 9-11.

Benn, C. (1981), *Attacking Poverty through Participation,* PIT Publishing, Melbourne.

Biddle, W. and Biddle, L. (1965), *The Community Development Process,* Rinehart and Winston, New York.

Bishop, A. (1994), *Becoming an Ally,* Fernwood Publishing, Halifax.

Brager, G., Specht, H. and Torczyner, J.L. (1987), *Community Organising,* Columbia University Press, New York.

Cain, R. (1993), 'Community Based AIDS Services: Formalization and Depoliticization', *International Journal of Health Services,* vol. 23, Fall, pp. 665-684.

Community Worker Group (1998), *Discussion Paper,* Community Worker Group, Toronto, January 7.

Cross Branch Community Worker's Group (1980), *Framework for the Eighties: Internal Report,* Children's Aid Society of Metropolitan Toronto, Toronto.

Cross Branch Community Worker's Group (1990), *Community Work Programme Report,* Children's Aid Society of Metropolitan Toronto, Toronto.

Cross Branch Community Worker's Group (1992), *Community Work Programme Report,* Children's Aid Society of Metropolitan Toronto, Toronto.

Dominelli, L. (1988), *Anti-Racist Social Work,* Macmillan, London.

Freire, P. (1970), *Pedagogy of the Oppressed,* Seabury Press, New York.

Illich, I. (1972), *Deschooling Society,* Harper and Row Publishers, New York.

Kahn, S. (1982), *Organising,* McGraw-Hill Book Company, New York.

Kretzman, J. and McKnight, J. (1993), *Building Communities from the Inside Out,* Centre for Urban Affairs and Policy Research, Evanston, Illinois.

Kelleher, P. and Whelan, M. (1992), *Dublin Communities in Action,* Combat Poverty Agency, Dublin, Canada.

Lakey, B., Lakey, G., Napier, R. and Robinson, J. (1995), *Grassroots and Non Profit Leadership*, New Society Publishers, Philadelphia, PA.

Lakey, G. (1987), *Powerful Peace Making*, New Society Press, Philadelphia, PA.

Lee, B. (1992), *Pragmatics of Community Organisation*, Second edition, Commonact Press, Mississauga.

Lee, B., McGrath, G., Moffatt, S, Usha, K.G. (1996), 'Community Practice Education in Canadian Schools of Social Work', *Canadian Social Work Review*, vol. 13, no. 2, pp. 221-236.

Mayo, M. (1977), 'Community Development or Social Change' in R. Bailey and M. Brake (eds), *Radical Social Work*, Edward Arnold, London, pp. 129-143.

MacIntyre, E. (1993), 'The Historical Context of Child Welfare in Canada', in B. Wharf (ed), *Rethinking Child Welfare in Canada*, McClelland and Stewart Inc., Toronto.

McKnight, J. (1996), *The Careless Society: Community and its Counterfeits*, Basic Books, New York.

McQuaig, L. (1995), *Shooting the Hippo*, Penguin Books, Toronto.

Mowbray, M. (1985), 'The Medicinal Properties of Localism', in R. Thorpe and J. Petrochina (eds), *Community Work or Social Change?*, Routledge and Kegan Paul, London.

Moyer, B. (1990), *The Practical Strategist*, Social Movement Empowerment Project, San Francisco.

Murphy, C.G. (1954), *Community Organisation Practice*, Houghton, Mifflin Company, Boston.

Newbury, D. (1989), *Stop Spadina: Citizens Against an Expressway*, Commonact Press, Toronto.

Oswin, H. (1984), *Community Development Work in Child Welfare*, Unpublished Master's Research Project, McMaster University, Hamilton.

Piven, F.F. and Cloward, R.A. (1977), *Poor People's Movements*, Pantheon Books, New York.

Plant, R. (1974), *Community and Ideology*, Routledge and Kegan Paul, London.

Prevention Team (1997), *Prevention Team Framework*, Children's Aid Society of Metropolitan Toronto, Toronto.

Repo, M. (1977), 'The Fallacy of Community Control', in J. Cowley, A. Kaye, M. Mayo and M. Thompson (eds), *Community or Class Struggle*, Stage 1, London, pp. 47-64.

Rice, J. (1990), 'Volunteering to Build a Stronger Community', *Perceptions*, vol. 14, no. 4, Autumn, pp. 9-16.

Rifkin, J. (1995), *The End of Work*, G.P. Putnam's Sons, New York.

Ross, M.G. (1972), *Community Organisation*, Second edition, Harper and Row Publishers, New York.

Rothman, J. and Tropman, J.E. (1987), 'Models of Community Organisation and Macro-Practice Perspectives: Their Mixing and Phasing', in F.M. Cox, J.L. Erlich, J. Rothman and J.E. Tropman (eds), *Strategies of Community Organisation*, Peacock Press, Ithaca, pp. 3-26.

Rubin, R.J. and Rubin, I. (1986), *Community Organisation and Development*, Merrill Publishing Company, Toronto.

Russel-Erlich, J. and Rivera, F.G. (1986), 'Community Empowerment as a Non-Problem', *Journal of Sociology and Social Welfare*, September, no. 3, pp. 451-465.

Saul, J.R. (1997), *The Uunconscious Civilisation*, Anansi, Toronto.

Thomas, D.N. (1983),'Participation in Politics and the Community', in D. N. Thomas (ed), *The Making of Community Work*, George Allen and Unwin Ltd, London.

Warren, R. (1983),'Observations on the State of Community Theory', in R. Warren and L. Lyons (eds), *New Perspectives on the American Community*, Dorey Press, Homewood Ill.

Wharf, B. (1997), 'Community Organisation: Canadian Experiences', in B. Wharf and M. Clague (eds), *Community Organising: Canadian Experiences*, University of Toronto Press, Toronto, pp. 1-14.

Wharf, B. (1979), 'Theory and Practice', in B. Wharf (ed), *Community Work in Canada*, McClelland and Stewart, Toronto, pp. 9-24.

5   The Children Act, 1989: A New Partnership with Parents?

MEHMOONA MOOSA-MITHA

Introduction

The Children Act passed in England in 1989, was hailed by many as 'the most comprehensive and far reaching reform of this branch of the law ever introduced' (Geoffrey Howe as quoted in White, 1989, p. vii). Its stated aim was to change the nature of child care in Britain by bringing 'together in a single coherent legislative framework the private and the public law relating to children' (DoH, 1991, p. 1).

In relation to the care of children being looked after by local authorities, the Act was to bring 'shifts in thinking' by social workers by incorporating an understanding of the research on best practice within their interventions. Moreover, the local authorities were instructed to promote the welfare of children by working in partnership with their families and the communities in which they lived.

This chapter considers the impact of the Act on the welfare of children. The analysis within it is based on the findings derived from research undertaken three years after the implementation of the Children Act, 1989 in one inner city borough of London. Sadly, the conclusions I reach indicate that there has been little, if any, improvement in the welfare of children in the care of that particular authority. According to this study, gaps in meeting children's needs supposedly addressed by the Children Act remain to be filled. Moreover, the new partnership the Act envisaged being developed between parents and the state also appears not to have materialised. Lack of adequate resourcing for both parents and local authorities appear to be responsible for this state of affairs.

The Children Act, 1989

A great deal of discussion has taken place about the changes effected by the Children Act, 1989 in terms of altering the power relationships between parents and the state or clients and workers. However, the conclusions are contradictory. Some writers such as Freeman (1992) have concluded that the Act is too non-interventionist because it gives too much power to the parents to the detriment of the children. Others, for example, Holman (1992) believe the Act to have increased the power of the state at the expense of the family. Another group which includes Williams (1997) feels that the Act attempts to strike a balance between the protection of the child and the freedom of the family. Reaching a consensus on this issue seems to be problematic although there is some acknowledgement that are varying degrees of power which exist within the family structure. However, for the purposes of this discussion, that is, my concerns with the power relations between parents and the state, I will treat the power differentials which occur within the family as less significant than those which occur around this polarity. Thus, I consider the family as one single entity and the state as another.

There appears to be a general agreement about some of the legislative changes brought about by the Act, even though their implications continue to be matters of controversy. These can be summarised as the following:

- an increased accountability on the part of the social workers to the legal system;
- an emphasis on the primary responsibility of the parents in bringing up children;
- an increase in the local authority's duties to provide services to families in need on a voluntary basis;
- a transfer of the legal powers and responsibilities of parents to local authorities only in the case where there was evidence of significant harm or the likelihood of such a harm being done to a child and only by following due legal process; and
- in the case of legal proceedings taken against parents, an increase in parental and children's entitlements to proper legal representation.

An examination of the above changes shows that two things have happened. Firstly, responsibilities to be undertaken by the family with minimal state intervention have increased. Secondly, the powers of local authorities have increased in relation to families when the likelihood of a child suffering significant harm is suspected by the social workers and affirmed by the courts. On the face of it, this is a reasonable enough arrangement, where if the family does not act as a unit to look after all its members including the children, the state is forced to intervene. However, this is considered the exception which is aimed at ensuring the welfare of the child. The state maintains a residual role that is largely preventive in situations in which children are experiencing need and a universal role that is interventionist when there is a suspicion that the child's life is endangered, that is, the possibility of 'coming to harm' is high.

The demarcation of the issues of child welfare into 'children in need' and 'children at risk' is a significant one. With the advent of the Children Act, the state's interventionist role in promoting the welfare of children has shifted its focus away from a wide range of child welfare issues whilst giving particular regard to child protection matters as a subset of this, to emphasising child protection by relegating more general child care concerns to a subsidiary place within the remit of ensuring the safety of the child (Parton, 1991).

This change in the focus of the role of the state is reflected in the increased powers and responsibilities placed upon families by the Children Act. As a result, a realignment has taken place in the relationship between the family and the state. Child care has become 'privatised' by drawing heavily on the parents' duty to provide care for their offspring. In other words, the family is looked upon as a consumer who may choose to use the services of the local authority for support in the privatised function of maintaining itself (Parton, 1991). This outcome is a consequence of the first three parts of the Act. These are concerned with the welfare of the child through the promotion of the rights and responsibilities of the family and the duties of the local authority to support the family in a voluntary capacity. This may include the local authority looking after children on a temporary basis when parental care has fallen down.

Part four of the Children Act, 1989, relates to the transfer of power and responsibility from the parents to the local authority where there exists the likelihood or evidence that the child will suffer significant harm by remaining in the family. The term 'likely to suffer significant harm' is deliberately left vague in the legislation so that the onus is on social workers to provide a definition of 'harm' and the likelihood of its existence to the courts. The power of the courts is increased by adjudicating on matters relating to the transfer of power from the family to local authority. The power of the local authority also increases when it is given primary responsibility in the everyday care decisions of the child. Unlike previous child care legislation, the family retains the right to challenge the courts' decision and the right to proper legal representation.

Perspectives on Child Welfare Policy

Perspectives on child welfare policy are essentially about two interrelated concepts: power and relationships. In child welfare situations, power relates to the notion of the state's ability to intercede in the lives of children and their families. It also refers to the question of the extent to which the role of state can be described as being interventionist versus being preventative, or the degree to which its activities can be considered universal as opposed to residual. Relationships define the nature of association between two parties. In the case of the state and a family, the relations between them are influenced by power (re)distribution or the extent to which power is shared, whether this be in a voluntary or involuntary manner, or a conflictual versus a consensual one.

The mechanism by which power relations are defined in the Children Act, 1989, is through the legalisation of the powers and duties placed on the state, the professionals and the family and their implication for the distribution of resources amongst them. Relationships are defined through the Act by its emphasis on the principle of partnership and the insistence on consensual decision-making through the use of work agreements between the family and local authority in the performance of their respective duties. Hence, a critique of the Children Act, 1989, must include the concepts of power and relationship and the shifts in these brought about by the Act.

Partnership

The Act intends that the relationship between the state and family is based on the principle of partnership. Although the word 'partnership' is not defined in the legislation and does not appear anywhere in the statutory legislation itself, it is cited as an underlying principle of the Act in the official guides to it (DoH, 1991). In those instances in which the local authority has a supportive role, partnership is defined in consensual terms. These guidelines also dictate that mutual agreements are to be reached between the parents who hold primary responsibility for looking after the child in their role as consumers and the local authority in its role as the provider of the service.

In cases of child protection, the Act assumes a partnership on unequal terms. For in these situations, parental responsibility is, to a large extent transferred, onto the local authorities. The family is no longer a consumer making a free choice as to which services they would like the local authority to provide for them and their children. Their power is relegated to a procedural one which has the capacity to challenge the course of events. The Family Rights Group suggest that the operative definition of partnership in this context should be considered in the following terms:

> Partnership is not about equal power, but about people working towards a common goal. It is about empowerment, about parents having sufficient information to be able to contribute to planning and to have some power to influence the outcome. Families do not want equality, and nor is that envisaged by the Children Act (DoH, 1991, vol. 1, p. 5).

To recapitulate, power relations between the state and families in need is shared on a consensual basis with the common goal of promoting the welfare of the child. In situations involving child protection issues, the power relations between the state and the family are characterised by inequality. For in these, the state has the greater power and the partnership becomes more adversarial because it is played out in court. Yet, this process, too, has as its common goal, the promotion of the welfare of the child.

This state of affairs is problematic because a consensual relationship in the first case can only be the result of a superficial definition of need. The structural context in which need occurs is ignored. Additionally, despite advocating a supportive role for the state for children in need, the British government resisted any attempts at linking legislation on child care with other social legislation like the Housing Act or the Social Security Act

(Parton, 1991). Moreover, child care legislation and the demands placed on social services to meet the needs of children are not linked to resource implications in other policy areas like housing. Yet, there is overwhelming evidence to show that most children in the care of local authorities have come from families that experience poverty and homelessness as well as discrimination on racial and cultural grounds.

The result of this approach is the privatisation of children's need with the responsibility to address that need firmly placed on individual families. The very public arena from which that need arises ignored. Furthermore, the resource implications for local authorities implementing the Act, is also limited by this definition of need. In the second process where state intervention occurs due to child protection issues, this privatised concept of need is further affirmed. Child abuse is seen as the failure on the part of the parents to look after their family and the state intervenes to take over that duty. Although present legislation is sensitive to the fact that parents have a right to challenge court decisions, in fact the present Children Act has actually increased and broadened the powers of state intervention through the Child Assessment Order and the Emergency Protection Order. For in these, the preponderant weighting of power lies in the hands of the state.

The Study

It is this privatised notion of need assumed in the Children Act, 1989, that this study examines by analysing the ability of a particular local authority to promote the welfare of children in their care over the period of three years since the inception of the Act. I do so by considering the outcomes of services delivered to children in its care and their impact on their well-being as 'children in need'. I utilise a needs analysis for children who are accommodated by or in the care of local authorities to ascertain the extent to which the Act enables them to meet the needs of children directly under their supervision. I use the Department of Health's definition and categorisation of need to evaluate service outcomes. This approach seeks to yield an understanding of the efficacy with which the Act enables local authorities to meet their own standards of care when promoting the welfare of children in their care.

Methodology

The study was quantitative in nature and used a survey questionnaire design. Three research assistants filled out the relevant questionnaires using case files as their main source of information. Two hundred and twenty three children in the teenage group of between the ages of twelve and eighteen were recorded as being looked after by the local authority in question during the month of November 1994. For twenty-three of these children, no information was available either because they had left the care system very soon after entering it or, in some cases, children were recorded twice using two different names. In the end, information on two hundred children was obtained and analysed.

The case files for each of these children were examined for information on demographic data as well as data on the needs of the children in the sample population. Children's needs were categorised according to the recommendation of the Department of Health. This gave the following categories of need for each child:

- health and development needs;
- emotional and mental health needs;
- needs based on family relationships;
- educational needs;
- identity needs;
- self-care skills and needs; and
- social presentation needs.

Once the information relating to these categories was collected, it was coded numerically for quantitative data analysis using the software package, SPSS (1985). Data analysis was then used to critique the findings of the study.

The findings of the research are depicted in the tables below. The first table (Table 1) refers to the age distribution of the young children who were being looked after by the local authority at the time that the study was undertaken. It reveals that the bulk of the children then in care were concentrated at the higher end of the age scale. The average age of the children entering the care system in this research was discovered to be about 10 years. This finding is consistent with those obtained in earlier studies. These have persistently revealed that over 50% of children in the care of local authorities are likely to be ten years of age or over (DHSS, 1985, 1988). In reflecting this trend, this study also highlights the difficulties that local authorities have in getting older children either back to their birth parents or adopted. Moreover, a majority of the children in this study had been in the care of the local authority for longer than two years. This, too, reflects the difficulties social workers have in securing sufficient alternatives for children in the longer-term.

Table 1   Age Distribution of the Young People in Care

Age	Number	Per cent
12	15	7.5
13	24	12.0
14	37	18.5
15	32	16.0
16	41	20.5
17	45	22.5
18	6	3.0
Total	**200**	**100**

The lengthy period that children spent in local authority care was a worrying development for it stands in direct contradiction with the spirit of the Children Act which aimed to promote the reunification of children with their families fairly quickly (s.23(6) and s.67(5)). My contention is that the failure of the local authority to direct its efforts to changing the circumstances in the life of the family of the child which led to the reception of the child in the first place, makes reunification harder to achieve.

Table 2 depicts the ethnic origins of the children in the sample which was the subject of this study. It reveals the high levels of black children which were in care at that time. In it, it is evident that black children

102

comprised nearly half the sample population. Moreover, black children were two and half times more likely to be looked after than their white counterparts.

Table 2   Ethnic Origins of the Children in Care

Ethnic Origins	Number	Per cent
White (U.K.)	35	17.5
White (Irish)	26	13.0
White (Other)	4	2.0
Black (African)	27	13.5
Black (Caribbean)	47	23.5
Black (British)	7	3.5
Black (Other)	16	8.0
Indian	10	5.0
Mixed Ethnic Origin	17	8.5
Other	9	4.5
Total	**198**	**99**

Other studies prior to the implementation of The Children Act, 1989, had noted the over-representation of black children in care (Rowe, 1984, 1989; Barn, 1993). The Children Act, 1989, sought to change this picture by promoting culturally sensitive practice. It placed a duty on local authorities to: provide for relevant cultural activities for children looked after, recruit day carers and foster carers from different racial groups and to take into consideration the child's racial origin and cultural and linguistic background in meeting children's needs or when making decisions around care plans (s.22(5), s.61(3) and s.74(6)). Yet, the number of black children in care remains disproportionately high. Data collected on the ethnicity of foster carers has shown that they come from similar backgrounds to the children in the majority of cases, so do the social workers working directly with the children. The assumption that culturally sensitive practice which ignores the structural socio-economic circumstances of the black communities living in Britain will, nonetheless, be sufficient in reducing the number of children entering the care system, is unfounded according to the experience of this sample population.

Children from 'Indian' ethnic groups were under-represented in this sample. Again, this finding is not dissimilar to that evidenced in Rowe's (1989) study. It also showed children from Asian backgrounds were under-represented in care situations. Although previous studies had shown children from mixed racial or ethnic backgrounds to be highly over-represented in the care system, this study did not find that to be the case. The findings in this study, therefore, differed from others in this respect. However, it is not clear that the Act was responsible for this outcome.

Table 3 focuses on the legal route which was used to bring the children in this study into the care system. Sadly, the bulk of them came through the compulsory route (section 31). This finding goes against the spirit of the 1989 Act in which there is an emphasis on preventing the use of care orders (s.31) as much as possible and promoting voluntary arrangement (s.20) by having practitioners work in partnership with parents (schedule 2, para7).

Thus, in this sample population, the majority of children entered the care system without parental agreement. Studies conducted prior to the implementation of the Children Act have shown a similar pattern (Barn, 1990). It seems that state intervention is set up to be truly effective largely in its coercive role, in the arena of child protection issues. The assumption that families will voluntarily participate in a supportive arrangement with local authorities in the caring of their children is not backed up by data collected in this study.

Table 3   Legal Route for Entry into Care

Legal Status	Number	Per cent
Section 20	74	37.0
Section 31	111	55.5
Section 38	4	2.0
Other	11	5.5
Total	**200**	**100**

Profile of Child Welfare

Need is a difficult concept to operationalise for its actualisation relies on contentious value judgements about what is appropriate for people to have. Moreover, its definition is deeply implicated in the playing out of specific power relations which arise from differences in the ideologies and material resourcing held by each of the contesting parties engaged in the interaction involved in defining need. The state, parents and children may each have differing views about what constitutes need and this may set the scene for difficulties between them. However, the law attempts to set legal parameters within which their negotiations over need are played out, although this does not always solve the problems which they may encounter.

The Children Act broadly defines 'children in need' as children who are not likely to achieve or maintain a 'reasonable standard of health and development' (s. 17). This definition of need is problematic, particularly as it is usually stigmatising and taken to mean that the children concerned have received a poorer standard of care than that expected by the professionals who pass such opinions. Thus, it reflects the greater power held by practitioners.

A close examination of each category of need as defined by the local authority follows. The Department of Health has added to this definition by categorising need into seven areas which have been mentioned previously. Each of these is examined in the following sections. However, it was not possible to collate information on all seven categories from the children's files that were examined in this study because social workers had recorded very little information about two of them - identity and social presentation needs. Nonetheless, the information which was available enables a comparison to be made between the levels of need local authorities met before the 1989 Act and that achieved three years after its implementation.

Table 4 below portrays the extent to which the general health and development needs of the children have been met.

Table 4   The Health and Development Needs of Children in Care

Health and Development	Yes		No		Don't Know	
	No.	%	No.	%	No.	%
Good physical health	154	77.0	35	17.5	12	6.0
Disability	16	8.0	174	87.0	10	5.0
Prone to infection	1	0.5	189	94.5	10	5.0
Asthma	15	7.5	175	87.5	10	5.0
Failure to thrive	1	0.5	189	94.0	10	5.0
Enuretic	3	1.5	187	93.0	10	5.0
Pregnant	2	1.0	188	94.0	10	5.0
Other health issues	43	21.5	150	74.5	6	3.0
No information	12	6.0	186	93.0	1	0.5

The definition of social need assumed in the Act depends on the accessibility of information which the state's agents can use to intervene in a supportive role. As can be seen in the above table on the general health needs of children, a large amount of information on health and health related issues were not available for 5% of the community. Moreover, 62% of the children did not have medical records on file despite the requirement in the Children Act to identify their needs in this area (schedule 2, para.1). And, 42% of the children did not have medical histories on file, either. Hence the results presented under this category may actually understate the level of need of the sample population.

The rate at which disability is found amongst children in care in this study reflects approximately the same levels as those found in previous studies (Thoburn and Rowe, 1988). Although the rate of infection recorded in this study was rather low, asthma recorded at 7.5% is higher than that found within the general population. The rate at which enuresis is found in this study is considerably lower than that of previous ones. There was also a very low frequency recorded of girls who were pregnant in this sample population. This indicates a departure from previous studies.

Table 5 depicted below focuses more closely on the mental and emotional needs of the children studied.

Information on the area of the mental and emotional needs of children was more readily extracted from the case files than was possible for the previous one. Nearly 43% of the children in the sample population were described as 'not well-adjusted'. This finding is consistent with another study conducted by Wolkind about a decade earlier. Using the Bristol School Adjustment guide, Mapstone (1969, quoted in Wolkind) had reported that one third of her sample population were 'badly adjusted'. This figure she considered to be three times higher than that prevalent in the general population. The figures obtained from this study of a London borough reveal that the rates for children who are 'badly adjusted' are higher than those indicated in previous ones.

Ackhurst (1975) found similar rates of acting out and aggressive behaviours as this study. The numbers of children looked after by local authority showing depressed or withdrawn behaviours as well as drug addictions has consistently been commented upon by various authors and continues to be a problematic area according to the figures provided through this study.

Table 5   The Mental and Emotional Needs of Children in Care

Mental and emotional needs	Yes		No		Don't Know	
	No.	%	No.	%	No.	%
Well adjusted	108	54.0	86	43.0	6	3.0
Psychiatric disorder	11	5.5	185	92.5	4	2.0
Learning difficulty	17	8.5	179	88.5	4	2.0
Acting out/aggressive	65	32.5	131	65.5	4	2.0
Stealing/lying	40	20.0	156	78.0	4	2.0
Depressed/withdrawn	23	11.5	173	86.5	4	2.0
Self-mutilation	3	1.5	193	96.0	4	2.0
Promiscuity	2	1.0	194	97.0	4	2.0
Addiction to drugs	12	6.0	184	92.0	4	2.0
Solvent abuse	2	1.0	194	97.0	4	2.0
Other issues	30	15.0	166	83.0	4	2.0
No information	4	2.0	196	98.0	n.a.	n.a.

Although mental and emotional problems in children may not be the result of being looked after by social services, nevertheless, poor mental health continues to afflict the young when in the care of local authority to a significant degree. The changes in the legislation seemed to have had little impact on the prevalence of such activities.

Families are important to children. Table 6 which follows demonstrates the extent to which there was interaction between children and their birth families and significant others.

Partnership with the family, particularly when relating to children in need depends on social workers being able to facilitate continual contact with their family. The Children Act recognises this and makes it a duty of local authorities to promote contact between children and their birth families (schedule 2, paras. 10,15,16). The findings of this study show that only 40% of the children had regular contact with the mother, less than a third had regular contact with the father and nearly half of them did not have regular contact with the siblings. This is consistent with the DHSS

(1995) study, *Looking after children*, which found that 46% of the children studied needed work done on promoting links with their families.

Table 6   Family Relationships Sustained by Children in Care

Family Relationship	Regular		Occasional		None	
	No.	%	No.	%	No.	%
Contact with mother	81	40.5	62	31.0	57	28.5
Contact with father	51	25.5	39	19.5	110	55.0
Contact with siblings	102	51.0	41	20.5	57	28.5
Contact with extended family	96	48.0			104	52.0
Contact with significant others	32	16.0			168	84.0

Yet, the carrying out of such work is difficult to guarantee. Sometimes, families lack the resources for retaining contact with their children. At other times, children may be placed a long distance away from their families because of the (lack of) availability of placements. Local authorities who hare closing down local residential provisions, for example, are having to place children requiring residential services out of area. This increases the burden parents, particularly if they are poor, carry in maintaining contact with their children for resources to assist them in this matter are extremely tight.

The educational needs of children in care can suffer if they are not adequately addressed. This can occur as a result of poor schooling environments, lack of appropriate adult stimulation and poverty. The absence of appropriate links between social services departments and the schools can also exacerbate this situation. Poor co-ordination and slip-shod communications between these two agencies can create substantial problems for children. Teachers can be an important source of information about a child's behaviour and his or her relationships within the family.

They can act as an early warning system for social workers. Yet, they often fail to tell social workers about their concerns because the links for sharing such information are not well-developed. Ironically, schools are getting involved in social work interventions when they are providers of a universal service which does not carry a stigma. Table 7 indicates the levels of educational attainment reached by the children included in this study.

Table 7   The Educational Needs of Children in Care

Educational Achievement	Yes		No		Don't Know	
	No.	%	No.	%	No.	%
Average or better performance	97	48.5	71	35.5	32	16.0
Delayed language development	12	6.0	172	86.0	16	8.0
Non-attendance	16	8.0	168	84.0	16	8.0
Irregular attendance	12	6.0	173	86.5	15	8.0
Statemented	31	15.5	153	76.5	8	4.0
Excluded	24	12.0	161	80.5	15	8.0
Suspended	4	2.0	181	90.5	15	8.0
Behavioural problems	24	12.0	161	80.5	15	7.5
Other issues	28	14.0	157	78.5	15	7.5
No information	15	7.5	185	92.5		

When looking in the files for information on the educational needs of children, the researchers found that much of this was lacking. There were 15 children who had absolutely nothing on file regarding their educational achievements or needs and 52%, nearly half the children in the sample population, had no school reports in their records.

As can be seen from the above table, nearly a third of the children within the sample population were recorded as having performed at less than average level. However, 48 % of the children currently attending an educational institution and who had information about their educational attainments on file performed at less than the average level. According to Rowe et al (1984), 15 % of the general population is considered to perform at 'below average' level. Thus, children in the study I conducted were three times more likely to be under-achievers. Again, this lack of educational achievement has often been noted in previous research. From this I conclude that the Children Act, 1989, has not had much impact in addressing the educational needs of children looked after in this sample population.

Low educational attainment hinders children's future prospects. Additionally, children who have been in care are seldom adequately prepared for entry into the adult world. Yet, moving from being in care into the outside world is an important period of transition between childhood and adulthood. Many practical skills have to be learnt in setting oneself up as an independent householder. These include negotiating with other people, learning how to network and reciprocate in relationships, and practical activities like paying bills, getting around town, finding a job, rising on time to get to work and feeding oneself a healthy diet amongst other things. The enormity of looking after oneself can be scary and many young people are put off by the thought unless they are adequately supported in this task. Parents often help their offspring ease the load. Other members of the family can also share this task. Matters become more complicated for young people who have lost contact with their (extended) families while they are in care because the state usually provides very little as an alternative once children leave its remit.

Table 8 reveals the skills that the children in the study had acquired to survive outside of the care setting.

Table 8   **The Self-care Needs of Children in Care**

Self-care Skills	Yes		No		Don't Know	
	No.	%	No.	%	No.	%
Appropriate self-care skills	116	58.0	42	21.0	43	22.5
Cooking skills	133	66.5	25	12.5	42	21.0
Budgeting skills	133	66.5	28	14.0	39	19.5
Public transportation know how	134	67.0	14	7.0	52	26.0
Other issues in self-care	41	20.5	126	63.0	33	16.5
No information on file	38	19.0	162	81.0		

It is particularly important that sixteen and seventeen year olds identify the skills they have for self-sufficiency as they prepare for independent living as adults. Bonerjea (1990) found that teenagers leaving care did not have the self-care skills needed to live on their own. Lack of information for one fifth of the sample population I studied continued to be a problem in assessing achievements in this area. According to my research, just over half the children had been assessed as having appropriate self-care skills for their age. It should be noted that in the 'other' category, one of the most frequent responses was the difficulty teenagers had experienced in utilising decision-making skills. Many of the respondents indicated that teenagers did not know how to participate in decision-making, particularly as it related to their long-term plans. This is a significant finding for this study because a working partnership presupposes mutual decision-making skills. Besides indicating the shallowness of the state's commitment to partnership, this point also demonstrates how few independent rights children can genuinely exercise.

Responding to Social Need

This study has examined the level of social need experienced by children looked after by one local authority. In the discussion so far, I have argued that the definition of social need assumed in the Act has relegated intervention by the state to a residual level. This has rendered social work intervention ineffectual in meeting the needs of the children.

The findings of this study strongly endorse this contention. It shows that using the official criteria by which to define need found in research conducted prior to the inception of the Children Act, 1989, most of the patterns of need, remain unchanged three years after the implementation of the Act. The most evident of these shortcomings are: information on key areas of need not being available; identification of need not always being possible; children continuing to enter the care system through non-voluntary arrangements; and, the continued over-representation of black children in care. In spite of the fact that the local authority in question has established a complaints department for families to express their dissatisfaction, and a review department to create a forum for joint decision-making, the level of needs experienced by children in care has not dropped substantially. Family participation in the decision-making involving children's needs without the power to voice a definition of need has led to a form of partnership which has had little impact in promoting the welfare of children.

The powers and duties placed on the family through this legislation are indeed greater than those found in previous legislation. However, this also differs in being premised on a privatised, consumerist concept of relationships in society. The market based ethos of the Act does not accurately reflect the nature of the relationship between the family and the state, as families in need do not have the material resources assumed of a consumer, which allows for the free choice in the purchase of services. To assume a capacity which is not present for families with children in need is to ignore the real nature of power relations in a society in which the resource-holders are the local authorities themselves. Hence, the sharing of power accorded by the legislature does not translate into a sharing of resources as can be seen in the limited definition of need applied by the local authorities when servicing need. Moreover, Williams (1997) found that parents perceived review meetings where joint participation on child care plans are made as a 'rubber stamping exercise'. The local authority generally decided what services it could afford to offer regardless of need or parental choices - a view which has subsequently been upheld by the British courts. Consequently, parents have felt that they have had very little power to alter decisions reached by the local authority acting through its social workers.

As Arnstein (quoted in DoH 1991, vol. 1, p. 5) comments:

> Participation without redistribution of power is an empty and frustrating process for the powerless. It allows the policy-holders to claim that all sides were considered but makes it possible for only some of those sides to benefit. It maintains the status quo.

Local authorities themselves face increasing constraints on resources as a result of the continual erosion in the role of the local state post-Thatcher. The Children Act, 1989, has been 'set in the context of increasing poverty, social polarisation and a fundamental re-evaluation of welfare provision' (Williams, 1997, p. 181). The wider socio-economic context in which the Act is situated makes it even less possible for local authorities to provide services to families in need in spite of their broadened powers to offer services to these families on a voluntary basis. This drives local authorities further into maintaining their child protection role for this is a responsibility that they cannot avoid while simultaneously limiting their efforts in addressing issues of social need and ignoring the wider resource implications of responding to identified need.

Conclusion

This study shows that the Children Act, 1989, has not resulted in a significant improvement in services to 'children in need' and in the care of local authorities. The concept of need assumed in the Children Act, 1989, had resulted in superficial changes in promoting the welfare of children requiring public assistance. The Act does not pay due regard to the unequal power relations that exist between the family and the state. It assumes a consensual model of partnership and ignores the constraints on resources experienced by both families and the state. Thus, there has not been a new partnership created between parents and the state. Moreover, the findings in this study show that operating on the false assumptions of parental material largesse works to the detriment of children in the care of local authorities. Consequently, their needs can remain unmet.

References

Ackhurst, B. A. (1975), 'The Prevalence of Behaviour Problems among Children in Care', *Educational Research*, vol. 17, pp. 137-142.

Barn, R. (1990), 'Black Children in Local Authority Care: Admission Patterns', *New Community*, vol. 16, no. 2, pp. 14-28.

Bonnerjea, L. (1990), *Leaving Care in London*, London Children's Regional Planning Committee, London.

Department of Health (DoH) (1991), *The Children Act, 1989: Guidance and Regulations,* vols. 1 and 2, HMSO, London.

Department of Health (DoH) (1995c), *Looking After Children*, HMSO, London.

Department of Health (DoH) (1995d), *Social Work Decisions in Child Care: Recent Research Findings and their Implications*, HMSO, London.

Department of Health and Social Security (DHSS) (1985), *Review of the Child Care Law: Report to Ministers of an Inter-Departmental Working Party*, HMSO, London.

Department of Health and Social Security (DHSS) (1988), *Children in Care: Memorandum Laid Before the Social Services Select Committee*, HMSO, London.

Freeman, M.D.A. (1992), *Children, their Families and the Law: Working with The Children Act,* Macmillan, London.

Holman, B. (1992), 'Flaws in Partnership', *Community Care*, 20 February, pp. 12-16.

Parton, N. (1991), *Governing The Family: Child Care, Child Protection and the State*, Macmillan Education Ltd, London.

Rowe, J., Kain, H., Hundleby, M. and Keane, A. (1984), *Long Term Foster Care*, BAAF/Batsford, London.

Rowe, J., Hundleby, M. and Garnett, L. (1989), *Child Care Now*, BAAF, London.

Thoburn, J. and Rowe, J. (1988), 'Research: A Snapshot of Permanent Family Placement', *Adoption and Fostering,* vol. 2, no. 3, pp. 37-51.

Thoburn, J., Lewis, A., Shemmings, D. (1995), *Paternalism or Partnership: Family Involvement in the Child Protection Process*, HMSO, London.

White, R. and Lowe, N. (1991), *The Children Act, 1989: Working in Partnership with Families: A Reader*, vol. 1, HMSO, London.

Williams, M. (1997), *Parents, Children and Social Workers: Working in Partnership under the Children Act, 1989,* Avebury, Aldershot.

Wolkind, S. (1979), *Medical Aspects of Adoption and Foster Care,* Heinneman Medical Books, London.

6 Family Group Conferences: A Challenge to the Old Order?

SHIRLEY JACKSON AND PAUL NIXON

In 1989, two major pieces of child care legislation were completed on opposite sides of the world: the Children, Young Persons and their Families Act was enacted in New Zealand; and the Children Act was passed in England and Wales.

The New Zealand Act had come about after major dissatisfaction with the prevailing means of dealing with children and young people deemed to be at risk of abuse or committing offences. A realisation was dawning that the practice in the 1960s, 1970s and early-1980s, of intrusive state intervention often resulting in the removal of children from home and replacing their family and community with stranger carers and institutions, had not been the envisaged solution to these problems. Permanency philosophy became equated with better professional organisation and securing permanent alternative placements for children, principally adoption. Children were seen as belonging to nuclear families. Wider family members were not considered in planning and often rejected as alternative caregivers on flimsy grounds (Wilcox et al, 1991). The previous legislation, the Children and Young Persons Act 1974, had provided a means for police and social workers to bring to court complaints regarding children in need of care, protection and control. A seminar during the International Year of the Child in 1979, reported that within this framework there were some serious inadequacies, notably a lack of co-ordination of services, an inadequate administrative framework, insufficient training for professionals and a lack of services (Geddis, 1979). An imported model of multi-disciplinary child protection teams was envisaged based on practice from abroad (Schmidt, 1978).

At the same time, there was a growing recognition that out-of-family placements of children were sometimes unstable and detrimental to the child's welfare, with children in care growing up with a sense of loss and displacement (Millham et al, 1986; McKay, 1981; Von Dadelzen, 1987). The treatment of young offenders in residential care was also a cause for concern with accusations of racism and brutality (Hassall, 1996).

There was, therefore, a clamour for reform from a number of quarters. In New Zealand, this included that emanating from the indigenous Maori community. Maori leaders were questioning the over-representation of their young people in social welfare institutions. This over-representation parallels the significantly higher proportion of black and mixed-heritage children in England (Rowe et al, 1989). In addition, there were a number of other concerns being expressed at the time: The perceived disintegration in traditional family structures, a desire to move towards more 'open government' with greater community participation and accountability (Barbour, 1991); and criticism of social workers failing to involve extended family in the protection of children (Pilalis et al,1988). An inquiry was set up to pick up on expressions of concern regarding the monocultural nature of proposals in a draft Bill in 1986 which included the lack of attention given to prevention and family support, the view of 'professionals as experts'; and high-handed approach of some of the specialist child protection teams. This produced the influential report, *Puao-Te-Ata-Tu*, meaning 'daybreak' (Ministerial Advisory Committee, 1988), which outlined the Maori concerns and some potential solutions. A greatly modified Bill which took a 'family group perspective' was presented to parliament in 1989. The then Minister of Social Welfare noted:

> The Bill recognises that the well-being of children and young people is bound in with the well-being of their families (quoted in Tapp, 1990, p. 82).

The final result was the Children, Young Persons and their Families Act of 1989. This Act placed at the centre of its decision-making powers, the Family Group Conference which took the place of the child protection team in the original Bill. The Family Group Conference (FGC) became the prime decision-making body for both care and protection and youth justice proceedings (Hassall, 1996). The philosophy underlying this approach is one of family-centred and culturally-sensitive practice. The inclusion of the word 'families' in the title of the Act underlines the intention to strengthen and maintain family groups (Connolly, 1994). The family and state are seen as working in partnership to achieve the best outcome for the children, with the families given the primary responsibility for caring for their children and ensuring a sense of identity, through having a central role in decision-making, whatever their culpability (Maxwell and Morris, 1992). The Act's general objectives can be summarised as:

- promoting culturally-sensitive and accessible community services;
- assisting children, young people and their families to prevent children suffering harm; and
- ensuring young offenders are held accountable for their actions and given opportunities to develop in more socially acceptable ways (adapted from Maxwell and Morris, 1992).

The New Zealand government's briefing paper at the time of the Act's introduction describes succinctly the underlying beliefs inherent in the legislation as follows:

> The procedures...are based on the belief that, given the resources, the information and the power, a family group will make safe and appropriate decisions for children. The role of professionals such as social workers and doctors should not be to make decisions, but to facilitate decision-making, by providing information, resources and expertise which will assist the family group. Professionals will have a crucial role as resource people (quoted in Ryburn and Atherton, 1996, p. 17).

In 1989, a second major piece of child care legislation was completed, namely the Children Act 1989 in England and Wales. This piece of legislation developed as a result of disquiet about the way child care legislation and practice were failing children and young people in the system. The Cleveland Inquiry (1987) a couple of years earlier had highlighted the need to exercise caution in over-riding parents' and children's rights and had outlined some practices such as denial of contact when children are removed under compulsory emergency protection as excessive and in most cases detrimental. The findings of this inquiry were added to other research findings (Millham et al, 1986; Packman, 1986; Fisher et al, 1986; Berridge and Cleaver, 1987) outlining the inadequacies in the child care system of the time, particularly in relation to contact between children in care and their families, and the lack of concern given to overall child care planning (DOH, 1985; Millham et al, 1989).

The Children Act 1989 sought to strike a new balance between the role of family and state in the care of children. Its main emphases were:

- the paramountcy of the child's welfare;
- parents having primary responsibility for their children rather than rights over them;
- working in partnership with users of services, communities and other agencies with a preference for voluntary rather than imposed services;
- a presumption of consultation and involvement in decision-making processes for children, parents and other family members;
- inclusion for the first time of specific clauses to ensure consideration is given to a child's racial, cultural, linguistic and religious background; and
- a duty of the state to protect children where this is deemed necessary.

The government issued several volumes of guidance and associated principles in order to assist workers to implement these changes to practice (DOH, 1989, DOH, 1991). It does not take too much imagination to see the similarities between the drivers towards the changes in legislation in both of these countries and the resulting emphases in relation to future child care practice. Both countries now have a requirement to put into practice the principles underpinning the legislative framework. However, practitioners and families in New Zealand now have a much clearer means to achieve the new relationship and balance of power envisaged by the new legislation in each country. Despite the aim of partnership, the Children Act 1989 issues no fundamental challenges to the power of professionals in decision-making. Whilst practice may be changing, the pace and direction of that change is still principally in the control of the professionals. Ryburn (1994a, p. 11) writes:

> Without an approach that challenges the assumed right of professionals to determine both decisions and the process of decision-making, any of the other challenges in the Children Act to the central tenets of traditional permanency philosophy are likely to founder.

Whilst this may be a pessimistic view, it recognises the essential difference offered by the New Zealand system which has taken the power from professionals and given it back to families by means of legislating for Family Group Conferences. Past failure of social workers to work 'with' rather than 'on' families (Millham et al, 1986; Packman et al, 1986; Fisher et al, 1986) could be assumed to have come about because of a lack of will on the part of the professionals to work in partnership. Certainly, professionals dominate the decision-making structures organisationally and conceptually. However, it is equally likely that the uncertainty as to how to achieve this ideal rather than a lack of intention may have been at the root of the problem (Ryburn and Atherton, 1996). For social workers to involve families in decision-making, there has to a robust model to facilitate this ideal. But in England and Wales, this has not been provided. We take the view that the Family Group Conference in the New Zealand provisions provides a mechanism for putting into practice many of the good intentions contained in the legislation in both the New Zealand and the England and Wales.

Family Group Conferences

So What is so Fundamentally Different about a Family Group Conference?

Firstly, we should be clear what we mean by a family. The term has come to be equated with a narrow picture of a nuclear, 2 parent family with 2.4 children, although recent statistics show that the reality is somewhat different. Less than half of households in England and Wales live in this hegemonic stereotype (Office for National Statistics, 1997). However, for the purposes of Family Group Conferences, family has a much broader definition. It includes extended family members as well as non-relatives who are significant to the child or parents. It may mean one main carer or may include a whole extended family and significant others from the child or family's community.

The essence of a Family Group Conference is a process for placing the responsibility and the decision-making powers regarding child care matters back with the family. It requires the family, rather than the professionals, to decide how best to protect and care for the children (Nixon, 1992).

The Child Welfare Model

In New Zealand, the FGC is central to the legal process. In its use in England and Wales, the model has been kept essentially the same as in New Zealand practice, although local variations do occur in both countries (Thornton, 1993: Lupton and Stevens, 1997). In this model, there is a preliminary phase and three key stages to the FGC itself, as well as possible subsequent review meetings.

- *The preliminary phase* is the referral to an independent co-ordinator who convenes the conference. The family is identified, in consultation with the child and immediate carers. The co-ordinator spends time *preparing* the family and professionals for the meeting and negotiating which family members attend. The co-ordinator can exclude certain family members in the interests of the child, but exclusions are rare and need to be specifically justified. The family will be consulted on the arrangements, including time and venue, they would like for their FGC.

- *Stage 1* of the FGC involves professionals sharing information with the family about their concerns for the child. The co-ordinator chairs this part of the meeting, ensuring information is presented in an accessible form, including in the chosen language of the family, and resources which may assist the family are described by the professionals. On almost all occasions, there are more family members than professionals present and the family can ask questions and seek clarification from the professionals. The professionals then leave.

- *Stage 2* is time for the family to draw up a plan in private which takes into account the concerns they have heard in the first part of the conference. They have as much time as they need and food and drink is provided to assist the process. No record is made of these private family deliberations.

- *Stage 3* begins when the family has agreed a plan and they ask the co-ordinator and any remaining professionals to rejoin their meeting. The plan is presented to the professionals for their agreement and any requests for resources are negotiated. The only ground for refusing a plan is if it places the child at risk of significant harm. The family is then asked to reconsider, but if an adequate plan cannot be agreed, the matter is referred to court. This happens only extremely rarely (Thornton, 1993; Lupton et al, 1995; Crow and Marsh, 1997), (adapted from Morris, 1994).

The Youth Justice Models

We have defined child protection broadly in terms of child welfare, and child protection, in its narrower sense. However, the New Zealand legislation also included provision for young offenders and while child protection and youth justice services in many countries are separated, the division is not universally applicable. In others, youth justice has oscillated between being considered part of child welfare and separate from it. We will, therefore, outline briefly the developments in the use of Family Group Conferences in youth justice internationally. The model espoused above is not entirely appropriate to describe how the use of FGCs has developed in youth justice.

There are essentially 2 models in operation in youth justice (see Figure 1). The first model is broadly speaking similar to the child welfare model, except that the victim is also part of the process. In the preliminary phase, the co-ordinator will prepare not only the young person and family members, but also the victim and their supporter(s). The victim will be consulted on the venue and process of the FGC. The victim will contribute to Stage 1 of the Conference and describe the impact of the offence on their lives and their preferred recompense. They will withdraw with the professionals to give the family private decision-making time. They may be part of the final stage of the Conference. Apologies, compensation and other considerations may be given as part of the Conference (Thornton, 1993; Hampton Trust, unpublished information).

In the alternative model, developed in Australia and adopted in some other projects around the world, the process is much more firmly rooted in notions of restorative justice. The victim and offender and their respective families and communities are brought together to resolve the situation which the offence has created. A key difference in this model is that the co-ordinator stays throughout the conference and moderates the process. There is much more emphasis in this model on the restorative and healing effects of the process itself rather than the devising of a plan for future action, although compensation and reparation are likely outcomes in this model too (Jackson, 1998).

In addition to the concerns expressed regarding child welfare legislation and practice world-wide, there are also increasing calls for more attention to the marginality of the victim to judicial process, the need for greater accountability for young offenders and the desire to make families more responsible for the criminal actions of their children (Shapland, 1985; Wright, 1991; Home Office, 1997). Family Group Conferences have been seen as one way of countering these problems in current youth legal systems, including youth justice.

Developments in the Use of Family Group Conferences in England and Wales

From 1990, the Family Rights Group, an independent organisation based in London but with a national brief, obtained funding to develop the use of FGCs in child welfare in England and Wales. There were initially 6 agencies participating as pilot projects in a nationally co-ordinated and researched venture to introduce the method with some degree of consistency and co-ordination across areas. These represented urban and rural, statutory and voluntary organisations. Two failed to develop (Crow and Marsh, 1997) but subsequently, many local authorities and some voluntary organisations have adopted the model, with varying degrees of adherence to the core elements.

Hampshire developed one of the original pilot projects in Winchester and has subsequently adopted the model across the whole county. The model has been used successfully both in Hampshire and across the other pilot projects in a variety of cases including complex and difficult child protection cases (Lupton et al, 1995; Crow and Marsh, 1997).

In youth justice, progress in England and Wales has been much slower. The National Association for the Care and Rehabilitation of Offenders (NACRO) set up a national steering group to try to mirror the development in child welfare established by the Family Rights Group. Unfortunately, due to lack of specific funding, it has not been possible for NACRO to take a leading role in co-ordination to the same extent as the Family Rights Group in child welfare. Pilot projects for using Family Group Conferences in youth justice have not been successful in obtaining national funding, but a few projects have managed to attract funding mostly from within their local authorities, notably Kent and Hampshire. To date, projects in youth justice in England and Wales are at early stages in their development and evaluation.

There are also developments in a number of other countries, notably Australia, Canada (in relation to domestic violence), South Africa, Sweden and the United States.

Common Themes in Child Care

There are a number of common themes running through child care practice which are currently under debate and to which FGCs may have something to contribute, notably:

- Family involvement.
- Family decision-making.
- Family satisfaction.
- Victim satisfaction.
- Children and young people's involvement.
- Cultural sensitivity.
- Family responsibility.
- Protection.
- Reduced state intrusion.
- Continuity.
- Family support.
- Financial costs.

Family Involvement

Family involvement is an aim which has permeated child care thinking in many countries over recent years and is included as a fundamental principle in both the New Zealand and England and Wales legislative frameworks. Under the Children Act 1989, it is expected that family members will be consulted and their views taken into consideration about any decision affecting a child looked after by the local authority (s.22). Parents retain their parental responsibilities even when a care order to the local authority has been granted (s.31). There is an assumption of their attendance at child care reviews (Review of Children's Cases Regulations 1991 Regulation 7 (2)). It is also expected in child protection guidelines (Home Office, 1991, p. 43) that parents at least will be involved fully in child protection investigations:

> It cannot be emphasised too strongly that the involvement of children and adults in child protection conferences will not be effective unless they are fully involved from the outset in all stages of the child protection process, and unless from the time of referral there is as much openness and honesty as possible between families and children.

Contrary to many social workers' expectations and experience in involving family members in professionally-run meetings, there is clear evidence that family members do attend FGCs, even in the most difficult of circumstances. Maxwell and Morris (1993) found that almost all families members take an active part in FGCs and when matters are serious, more wider family are prepared to attend.

Generally speaking, the number of family attenders at FGCs has a wide range from 2 to 39, with an average of 6-7 (Renouf et al, 1990; Maxwell and Morris, 1993; Lupton et al, 1995; Crow and Marsh, 1997). This is in sharp contrast to research available on attendance at other planning meetings (Thoburn et al, 1995; Grimshaw, 1996). Whilst the research into attendance at child protection conferences is now somewhat outdated and attendance rates are likely to have increased. The Grimshaw (1996) research shows there is still room for improvement in involving family members in traditional decision-making processes.

Whilst attendance at meetings may have improved over recent years (DOH, 1995), meaningful involvement is not necessarily afforded by attendance alone (Barber, 1994). Family Group Conferences give families an opportunity to be central to the decision-making process. Unlike the arrangements for many child protection conferences (Thoburn et al, 1995), FGCs are designed to be sufficiently informal and relaxed at a time and venue most suited to the family with appropriately presented information from the professionals to make the meaningful involvement of family members more likely (Maxwell and Morris, 1992).

Testimony from family members from both New Zealand and UK research lends weight to these findings:

A great idea - we were really involved. It is an excellent idea to sort it out in the home and to involve families (parent, quoted in Maxwell and Morris, 1992, p. 14).

It was good getting the family together to think about the kids. They feel more involved now than they would have been if they had not come to the Conference (parent, quoted in Morris, 1995, p. 31).

More family-orientated and the decision rests with the family and everyone knows what's going on (parent, quoted in Lupton et al, 1995, p. 94).

Fantastic idea. It's the family that should have a say, not some government official (parent, quoted in Lupton et al, 1995, p. 94).

Family Decision-making

A concern from professionals about FGCs has centred around the ability of families involved in serious child welfare situations to make appropriate decisions, which sufficiently take into account the child's needs (Tapp et al, 1992). In fact, agreement is reached which is acceptable to the professionals in 90% of cases (Renouf, 1990; Thornton, 1993; Maxwell and Morris, 1993; Lupton et al, 1995). In the recent research summary of practice in England and Wales, in 74 out of 80 cases, family members produced agreed plans which were fully acceptable to the professionals and deemed to be in the best interests of the child (Crow and Marsh, 1997).

A fundamental premise of the FGC model is that whilst professionals may have expertise in general about families, members of any individual family are likely to hold more information collectively than any professional is likely to access (Ryburn, 1992; DOH, 1995b). It is also likely that they would be unwilling to share this information with a professional present. Hence, the emphasis in FGCs on private family decision-making time (Nixon, 1992). Practitioners in New Zealand at the forefront of introducing this way of working concluded:

The families are the best source of information on which decisions can be made. We realised how inadequate our own assessments had been (Wilcox et al, 1991, p. 9).

Families also often come up with much more imaginative solutions to situations than the workers had envisaged (Wilcox et al, 1991; Crow and Marsh, 1997).

It could be argued that these families were the less difficult to work with and that so called 'dysfunctional' families would not be capable of formulating appropriate plans. In New Zealand, the model has been used for all cases, which would have been worked on using traditional methods since 1989, and therefore the possibility of using easier cases is not evident. Voluntary referral has been used in child welfare pilots in England and Wales, but Crow and Marsh (1997) found that on the contrary, in some situations, social workers actually referred the families 'when other methods had failed', suggesting the model was used with more difficult families. The majority of professionals were pleasantly surprised at the ability of family members to draw up good plans for their children. Typical comments were:

> We actually did get people into the same room having a fairly amicable discussion, which given the various things that had happened previously, was quite a surprise (copied from Crow and Marsh, 1997, p. 13).

> I think the expectation of the meeting was that it was likely to be aggressive and very violent, but in fact, it wasn't at all (copied from Crow and Marsh, 1997, p. 13).

Ryburn (1992) argues that as social work involvement with families has often been through its weakest link, a deficit model of intervention has developed. Family Group Conferences focus on a family's strengths rather than deficit models of the family. Ryburn (1992) goes on to argue that the family, in its widest sense, is more motivated than any other social institution to care for and protect its children. With adequate resources, families are capable of finding solutions to their problems. Even if their plans do not work, the results are no more damaging to the welfare of the child than the outcomes of ineffective professional decision-making. Unsuccessful plans should be addressed by further family decision-making, just as professionals have had the opportunity to reformulate their failed plans in the past (Ryburn, 1992).

Family Satisfaction

Another key indicator of success in modern day social work is consumer satisfaction. Findings in relation to FGCs are impressive compared with parallel professional decision-making processes (DOH, 1995). Levels of family satisfaction in both child welfare and youth justice Family Group Conferences are high (Maxwell and Morris, 1993; Lupton et al, 1995; Crow and Marsh, 1997).

Overall satisfaction levels in the England and Wales projects were at 75-80% (Crow and Marsh, 1997). Initial satisfaction levels on the plans by family members in the Hampshire child welfare project showed that 86% of family members described the process as good or very good, with only 4% scoring it negatively. This had fallen a little, 4-6 months post-conference, although only 5 out of 42 followed up had changed from a satisfied to dissatisfied category (Lupton et al, 1995). In contrast, parents involved in the child protection system report the experience as devaluing and undermining (Cleaver and Freeman, 1995).

Victim Satisfaction

In youth justice FGCs, one of the key aims is victim involvement and satisfaction with the process. This is increasingly of concern to politicians and practitioners in the UK and elsewhere (Home Office, 1997; Walgrave, 1995; Wright, 1995). Victim satisfaction levels with traditional court-based processes have been low (Shapland et al, 1985; Davis et al, 1992). Raine and Smith (1991) found half to two-thirds dissatisfaction with court processes on a range of measures. FGCs have a significantly improved rate of satisfaction. In New Zealand, initially victims were not sufficiently central to the FGC process, and a half were not involved. Of those who were involved 60% found participation helpful, rewarding and positive (Maxwell and Morris, 1993). Improvements have been made in recent practice and whilst no more up to date research has been conducted, it is reported that victims are now more fully involved in the process (McElrea, 1995). In Australian pilot projects, victims were always more central to the process and victim satisfaction levels are reported to be extremely high (Moore, 1995).

Children and Young People's Involvement

Another key objective of the Children Act 1989 and current thinking in child care practice is around the issue of children's involvement in decision-making processes.

In relation to attendance, Crow and Marsh (1997) found that attendance by children and young people at FGCs was higher than for other forms of decision-making procedures (Thoburn et al, 1995; Grimshaw, 1996). In a New Zealand study, satisfaction levels for children and young people were not as high as for other family members (Maxwell and Morris, 1993). Some young people felt their family had made the decision rather than their having a real voice. However, in the most recent study in England, Lupton and Stevens (1997) found that children did participate more extensively than in traditional approaches and scored higher than adults on satisfaction measures regarding some parts of the process, that is, the private family decision-making time. In fact, 90% of children for whom FGCs were called found it easier to talk without the professionals present and none found it more difficult. This is in sharp contrast to children and young people's lack of sense of involvement in other processes (Mittler, 1992; Thoburn et al, 1995). Mittler (1992) in her survey of young people attending child protection conferences found that 100% experienced difficulty in expressing their views.

In youth justice, there is concern that young peoples' rights are not sufficiently safeguarded with FGCs held outside the court process. This has been particularly an issue for youth justice workers where FGCs are police-led (National Children and Youth Law Centre, 1995) and one which developing projects need to consider carefully.

Cultural Sensitivity

Awareness of the need for consideration of culture in child care practice is increasing and as previously stated, culminated in England and Wales in the first reference in primary legislation to the need to consider 'race', culture, language and religion in decisions about children looked after by the local authority (Children Act, 1989 s.22(5)(c)). Despite these provisions, services to ethnic minority groups are still unevenly distributed. Barn (1993) found that black children were still over-represented in admission to care and there were problems with assessment and engagement with families. Sinclair et al (1995) found that whilst there has been some progress with African-Caribbean families, there are still considerable barriers to working with Asian communities who comprise the largest minority population in England and Wales.

FGCs originated from pressure exerted by the indigenous Maori community in New Zealand for practice to reflect more accurately their traditional decision-making processes. It was the experience in New Zealand that there was scepticism about the effectiveness of this process for *Pakeha* (white settler) families (Atkin, 1989). These fears were not borne out and the practice has been equally successful for white as well as Maori families (Wilcox, 1991; Maxwell and Morris, 1993). Similarly, there has been doubt expressed by practitioners in England whether the model will transfer cross-culturally. Again these fears have not been borne out in research (Lupton, 1995; Crow and Marsh, 1997). The model has sufficient flexibility to allow families to run conferences in a way which suits their culture and traditions and to develop plans which attend to the child's needs in the context of their background and culture (Nixon, 1992).

Some difficulties in addressing the needs of some minority groups were found in New Zealand and these seemed to centre around two main themes. Firstly, inattention to the 'race' and cultural background of the co-ordinator and lack of appropriate interpreters and secondly insufficient culturally sensitive resources to enable the plans to be effectively put into place (Thornton, 1993). These findings have not been mirrored in UK research, although numbers are fairly small yet for comparative purposes (Crow and Marsh, 1997).

Family Responsibility

Giving primary responsibility for their children firmly back to families is one of the aims of both the New Zealand legislation and the Children Act 1989. As use of the term in the Children Act and subsequent legislation and political rhetoric has shown, the term 'responsibility' can have a double-edged meaning.

Whilst it seems right that responsibility should be given back to service users in a sense of empowering them to make decisions, it can also be seen as a means of ensuring they take the blame for societal problems. This has been particularly evident in the recent drive to increase a sense of family responsibility, particularly in relation to young offending (Home Office, 1997).

On the other hand, for people to exercise self-determination and choice over their lives, they need the responsibility that choice offers them. By widening the parameters of the family, the FGC widens the group who can take collective responsibility in decision-making for the child. The involvement of the extended family has often shared the responsibility for child care matters and increased the support to the original care givers (Hassall and Maxwell, 1991). However, the rhetoric of family responsibility can easily lead to a reduction of support from the state. If FGCs are to be truly empowering, a range of services must be available to families if they are to exercise genuine choice and responsibility for their children.

Protection

Fundamental to the use of FGCs is the belief and evidence that families do make plans that offer equal or greater protection than professional decision-making (Wilcox et al, 1991). As the vast majority of children caught up in the child protection process remain in their family and community, failing to work co-operatively with families is likely to increase the risks to the child (DoH, 1995a). Furthermore, the child protection process devotes most attention to the details of abusive incidents with correspondingly little time spent on finding solutions (Farmer and Owen, 1995). For too long, child protection work has been characterised by an overemphasis on child rescue and social control rather than problem solving and providing supportive services (Holman, 1988; Parton, 1991; Audit Commission, 1994). FGCs by contrast are based on a problem solving model which focuses on the child's needs in the context of their family and by taking a 'wide view', identifies the help needed to improve the child's circumstances.

It should be noted that there has been recent concern that the lack of attention to planning in current child protection procedures gives grave cause for concern about their ability to adequately protect children (Farmer and Owen, 1995). Crow and Marsh (1997) found that professionals thought children were protected by the plans made by the family. About 67% of social workers felt that the children were better protected than they would have been without the FGC and none felt children were less well protected.

There are also early indications of a reduction in re-abuse rates, comparing favourably with traditional methods from 16-25% in national research on traditional methods (DOH, 1995) to 6% in the FGC sample.

Reduced State Intrusion

Given the poor results (DHSS, 1985; Rowe et al, 1984), a reduction in intrusive state intervention in children's lives has become an aim of child care and youth justice services alike. Bullock et al (1993, p. 67) noted:

> For the great majority of children in care, family members are the most important resources available to social workers, for it is parents, grandparents, siblings and wider family who are likely to provide continuing and unconditional support. It may be true that some children in care reluctantly go back to relatives because they have nobody else. Nevertheless, whether professionals like it or not, almost all children in care will eventually be restored to their family and our perspectives and interventions need to accommodate that fact.

Alongside a history of some children being abused in foster homes, the 'Pindown' and Frank Beck inquiries have shown that stranger care can offer no guarantee of safety or security for children removed from their families (Levy and Kahn, 1991; Kirkwood, 1992). A reduction in removal from home and placement in 'stranger' care is becoming a clear aim of legislation which deems that children should be supported in the community (Children Act 1989, s.17) or if they cannot remain with parents, placed in the extended family as an alternative to the local authority providing accommodation (Children Act 1989, s.23(6); DOH, 1991). However, in spite of this requirement, Berridge (1997, p. 17) notes that fostering with relatives seems to have been seldom used and concludes that:

> this is particularly curious given that research has consistently reported very positive outcomes for children fostered with relatives.

In contrast, FGCs have dramatically reduced the numbers of young children and young people both in care and custody in New Zealand (Renouf, 1990; Maxwell and Morris, 1993). There are also indications from UK research that with the use of FGCs, there is an increase in the use of relatives as substitute carers as opposed to stranger placements (Crow and Marsh, 1997).

Continuity

As the Bullock quote above indicates, families often provide the most enduring relationships for young people despite being away from home. The importance of both a sense of continuity in a child's life and the maintenance of links between children away from home and their families is now extensively documented (Rowe et al 1989; Millham et al, 1986; Millham et al, 1989; Bullock et al, 1993). A study of young people leaving youth treatment centres (Little, 1993) found little attention was given to their relationships with families and others outside the institution. Yet, those with the poorest outcomes were not necessarily the gravest offenders but those who lacked roots and support systems. Wedge and Mantle (1991) identified the importance of sibling contact and Millham et al (1986) that of grandparents, uncles and aunts who were largely under-used, excluded and unsupported. Even in adoption, some form of continuing contact is likely to be beneficial to the child's sense of continuity (Ryburn, 1994b). There is, therefore, an increasing recognition of the human need for a sense of belonging and continuity.

Family Group Conferences offer an opportunity to provide a greater sense of continuity for children as, firstly, they are more likely to remain in the family; and secondly, a greater commitment to on-going support and assistance is reached through FGCs. Crow and Marsh (1997, p. 15) found:

> The plans of the great majority of the Family Group Conferences (94%) involved family members offering resources in terms of support and help, often in ways that could not have been predicted. Distant relatives often played as much of a part in making plans as those living nearby. The help ranged from telephone calls to see how things were going, through doing gardening or baby-sitting, accompanying a parent out socially, taking or collecting children from school, having children for the weekends or holidays, to looking after children full time. In all, 31 % of plans involved family members offering to care for children for some period of time.

Family Support

The Children Act 1989, was carefully constructed to provide a balance between child protection and family support (Hill and Aldgate, 1996). It was hoped that services would become less reactive and controlling (Packman, 1993) and more accessible to those in need without the associated stigma. Research had highlighted that many children entering care were highly disadvantaged, with disrupted family relationships, poverty and lack of social support systems (DOH, 1991) and that the reasons for many children entering the care system related as much to material deprivation and lack of family support as to wilful neglect or abuse (DHSS, 1985; Packman, 1986). Recent research findings (DOH, 1995) have given a clear impetus to practitioners and policy makers to refocus provision in this direction.

The Children, Young Persons and their Families Act 1989 also included a general objective of promoting the well-being of children by assisting families to prevent harm (Maxwell and Morris, 1992; Connolly, 1994). Crow and Marsh (1997, p. 10) conclude that FGCs:

> provide a way of locating the issue of child protection within the broader
> context and they may generate support and help for the family in a way that
> is effectively tailor-made for that particular child and that particular family -
> a service that is very hard to provide from official agencies.

Financial Costs

Many of the above comments could be considered to reflect issues of effectiveness of the service. However, cost-effectiveness is becoming an ever increasing concern in the current climate of financial restraint in social services (Home Office, 1997). Whilst research into cost-effectiveness which is conclusive is itself expensive and, therefore, has been beyond the scope of most researchers to date, there are some indications from research regarding the cost-effectiveness of FGCs. The introduction of FGCs is certainly not cost-free (Nixon, 1992; Crow and Marsh, 1997). In fact, they may in certain cases prove more financially costly (Lupton et al, 1995). However, there are indications both in child welfare and youth justice that they can provide cost reductions over time. In New Zealand, it was found that in only 20% of youth justice FGCs were there on-going costs for the state (Maxwell and

Morris, 1993). Crow and Marsh (1997) give some rough indications of cost reduction for FGC cases compared with likely outcomes without an FGC. It is certainly likely that there are cost reductions on services given the enormous cost of court proceedings and residential care. It is important, however, that financial savings are recycled to provide support for families in a positive and constructive way.

Dilemmas for Family Group Conferences

So far, the message has been essentially positive for the use of Family Group Conferences. However, there are some areas about which there are concerns and which are likely to cause difficulties regarding the use of FGCs. This paper will now address some of these issues.

Time Frames

There is a recognition both in child care legislation in England and Wales (Children Act 1989 s.1(2)) and in proposals regarding changes in youth justice that there is a need to avoid delay in relation to decision-making (Home Office, 1997). This has become such a problem that it takes an average of four and a half months for a case to go through the youth court system at present (Audit Commission, 1996). Given these problems, FGCs may offer a speedier alternative to traditional formal decision-making routes. In the early days in New Zealand, the average amount of time to arrange a conference was 36 days (Paterson and Harvey, 1991). In Hampshire, Lupton et al (1995) found the average was 24 working days. However, in youth justice in England and Wales, National Standards require certain time frames to be adhered to in the process such as reports in 3 weeks, and this may cause some difficulties for setting up an FGC within the required period. The Mason Report on the implementation of Family Group Conferences in New Zealand (Department of Social Welfare, 1992) was concerned that the need to meet tight deadlines meant that conferences were sometimes poorly organised and, therefore, the full benefit of the conference was not achieved. A common theme for FGCs is that well-prepared FGCs equate with greater family attendance and better quality of conference (Renouf, 1990; Paterson and Harvey, 1991; Maxwell and Morris, 1993) and this can take time to achieve. It would, therefore, be necessary to persuade local courts to extend their time periods and this may be difficult if current proposals for a financial penalty for courts not meeting targets were to be introduced (Home Office, 1997).

Monitoring

One of the assumed strengths of the FGC model is the increased likelihood that plans made by the family are more likely to be carried out by them than those imposed by professional decision-making processes (Barbour, 1991). In New Zealand, these plans are meant to be reviewed 'from time to time' (CYPF Act, 1989) but there is no statutory provision for regulating this monitoring process. The implementation of monitoring has been patchy (Renouf, 1990; Paterson and Harvey, 1991; Department of Social Welfare, 1991).

In England and Wales, there has been an ethical debate about the monitoring of families' plans. Given that FGCs are meant to be an empowering process, giving decision-making back to the family, it *may* be a retrograde step to then impose a system of monitoring by professionals. In general, FGCs here have tried to involve a family member as well as a professional to take the responsibility for monitoring and feedback if there are problems. However, research has shown that significantly, both families and professionals have failed to follow through all aspects of the original plans and this needs further attention (Lupton et al, 1995). However, in serious child protection cases, in England and Wales at present, there are still in operation the child protection procedures which act as a monitoring process if necessary. If these were to be superseded by FGCs, then more attention would need to be paid to systematic monitoring.

In the Hampshire youth justice project, monitoring of the plan is being undertaken by the project manager and sometimes by co-ordinators where appropriate, and is presented as a service to the family to ensure the resources in the plan have been able to be accessed.

Inconsistency

One of the drives behind the government guidance, *Working Together* (Home Office, 1991), was to achieve consistency of practice across authorities in relation to child protection work. There has been concern expressed in New Zealand that the lack of clear national practice standards for FGCs has led to uneven and idiosyncratic practice in different areas (Barbour, 1991; Maxwell and Morris, 1993). The current trend to introduce Family Group Conferences by means of pilot projects in England and Wales lends itself to differential practice here. It could be argued that this is not problematic providing key principles are adhered to and in fact one of the strengths of FGCs is their adaptability to different situations and family structures. However, in a child protection context, it may give cause for concern to return to ad hoc practices with little government regulation.

However, to put this in context, fairly recent research into the operation of child protection registers in England found great variation in registration rates which could not be explained by different abuse rates (Gibbons et al, 1995), so the intentions of *Working Together* and the decades of attention to improving the co-ordination and organisation of the child protection system, have been unable to achieve the goal of consistency. It may be unrealistic to expect or strive to make FGC practice consistent across areas.

Given the concern of advocates of the FGC model to maintain standards, the Family Rights Group with the support of the Department of Health has developed a training pack to set out some guidelines for developing FGC work. A key objective must be to establish the core principles of FGCs in the context of child care thinking. In practice, a framework will need to be established which ensures that those core principles are adhered to. Then, much like the FGC model itself, the key features of FGCs are the minimum standards/requirements, whilst still providing a reasonable degree of flexibility within the overall framework. FGCs, therefore, will be driven first and foremost, by principles and core values rather than by procedures. To over-standardise or proceduralise the approach would be likely to dilute its effectiveness and move it away from a family and community-led process to one that is again dictated by the state.

Resources

A current concern in child care centres on the dearth of flexible and varied resources available to meet families' needs. A pre-occupation with risk assessment and a forensic approach to social work has left little room for supportive services to develop. If FGCs are to be effective they will need to be able to access resources families view as meaningful and helpful.

It is very disempowering to be asked to make a decision, only to have the plan founder due to an inability to resource it. Families need clear information at the beginning of the Conference in order to make plans which are realistic. But, a severe lack of resources can hamper that decision-making process. Thornton (1993, p. 26) writes regarding the New Zealand experience:

> the provision of new community programmes and services does not yet match the emphasis in the Act of keeping children and young persons out of state care and diverted from the justice system. Reports of insufficient community resources and support services to meet the needs of young persons and families in both care and protection and youth justice have cropped up regularly.

FGCs will only achieve their full potential when local authorities have coherent, well-developed, family support strategies. There are some examples of good practice in this area, but they tend to be piecemeal and ad hoc, with great variation amongst local authorities on interpretations of which children are 'in need' and what they need (Aldgate et al, 1994). It is likely that if systematic records are kept of FGC plans, then this should help with the development of more meaningful community-based services. Moreover, the integration and development of involving service users in the development of children's service plans for local authorities, is likely to change the emphasis of resources to more supportive policies and services.

Disempowerment of Some Family Members

Critics of the FGC model have argued that it replaces paternalism by the state with patriarchy and can be used by abusive family structures to reinforce damaging forms of decision-making in a family (Atkin, 1989).

However, Lupton and Stevens (1997) found no evidence to suggest that female members of the family group were less active or more vulnerable participants within the FGC process overall, although they were more inhibited by the information giving stage. They suggest that this may be due to the tendency of professionals to focus on the needs or perceived shortcomings of mothers rather than other family members. However, women scored highest on overall satisfaction with the FGC plan outcomes at the end of the FGCs and it is possible, that in the context of the wider family, responsibility and power will be more evenly distributed. It is also the case that many women have felt empowered by the FGC process. In the context of the wider family, it has been more difficult for the power of secrecy to operate and women have been able to establish coalitions across the family network in order to protect the children better (Ryburn and Atherton, 1996).

Professional Power

Wilcox et al (1991, p. 8) found that:

> The major practice hurdle was to relinquish the power of final decision to the family. This had to be done in spite of personal or professional points of view. We needed to learn our role was information giving; we gathered and provided all information to the family group in order for them to make an informed decision...the real movement came when we had committed ourselves to support and resource family decisions even when we did not personally agree with them.

Clearly there is a *different* professional role needed in relation to working in partnership generally and to FGCs specifically. This is likely to be the most major challenge to social workers and other professionals used to having a powerful decision-making role. FGCs require professionals to take a more enabling and facilitative approach and to be flexible and responsive to the expressed views of the family. This may lead to professionals who are uncomfortable with the ethos of Family Group Conferences putting up resistance to referring a family for an FGC. Whilst in England and Wales the power for referral to FGC rests with professionals, there is likely to be differential practice, based largely on unfounded professional concern rather than on real difficulties in using FGCs for a particular family.

However, it does not necessarily follow that by giving away power, professionals will feel disempowered; quite the opposite. Both Thornton (1993) and Lupton (1995) found a high degree of professional satisfaction and sense of empowerment by the process.

Conclusion

Family Group Conferences present a radically different way of working with families. The most significant difference is the site of decision-making power, transferred from professionals to families.

The evidence so far in both New Zealand and England and Wales is that FGCs work. However, their development is still at an early stage and therefore, ongoing careful monitoring of their development is required. They are working against the odds. All the current child welfare systems are predicated on a deficit model of families with professionals as the experts about their problems. FGCs provide a distinct challenge to the predominant way of working and thinking.

It is very likely that there will be a reactionary backlash to their use. This has been the experience in New Zealand and is likely to occur in England and Wales too, probably the first time something goes seriously wrong after an FGC has taken place. FGCs pose a fundamental threat to professional power and consequently, there will be those eager to find a reason to discredit them. This model of working challenges the foundations on which professional social work are based and it requires social work to change its role to one of empowering users. 'Can social work survive?' has been a question threatening the social work profession in Britain for at least two decades. Recent changes to their role in care management has heightened the awareness of the precarious place of the profession. Social work will improve its chances of survival if it is willing to change to being a service which is really user and family friendly.

FGCs represent a general value and attitude which respects families and communities and they should not be viewed as either another professional hoop families need to jump through in order to access services, or as a 'technical gizmo' bound to provide the required results. They should be seen to reflect an overriding attitude which should be used in all child care policies and practice. Let us not find in a few years time that FGCs get used by practitioners to fall foul of the 'DATA syndrome', a term coined by Peter Marsh, of the University of Sheffield, to say with regard to empowering users, 'We're using Family Group Conferences; so we're Doing All That Already!'

References

Aldgate, J., Tunstill, J., Ozolins, R. and McBeath, G. (1994), *Family Support and the Children Act: The First Eighteen Months - A Report to the Department of Health,* University of Leicester, School of Social Work, Leicester.

Atkin, W.R. (1989), 'New Zealand: Children versus Families - Is there any Conflict?' *Journal of Family Law,* vol. 27, pp. 231-40.

Audit Commission (1994), *Seen but not Heard,* HMSO, London.

Barber, C. (1994), *Playing by the Rules: An Evaluation of Child Protection Services in Hampshire,* Hampshire County Council, Winchester.

Barbour, A. (1991), 'Family Group Conferences: Context and Consequences', *Social Work Review,* vol. 3, no. 4, pp. 5-6.

Barn, R. (1993), 'Black and White Care Careers: A Different Reality', in P. Marsh and J. Triseliotis (eds), *Preverntion and Reunification in Child Care,* Batsford, London.

Berridge, D. and Cleaver, H. (1987), *Foster Home Breakdown,* Blackwell, Oxford.

Berridge, D. (1997), *Foster Care: A Research Review,* HMSO, London.

Bullock, R., Little, M. and Millham, S. (1993), *Going Home: The Return of Children Separated from their Families,* Dartmouth, Aldershot.

Connolly, M. (1994), 'An Act of Empowerment: the Children, Young Persons and their Families Act 1989', *British Journal of Social Work,* vol. 24, pp. 87-100.

Crow, G. and Marsh, P. (1997), *Family Group Conferences, Partnership and Child Welfare: A Research Report on Four Pilot Projects in England and Wales,* University of Sheffield Partnership Research Programme, Sheffield.

Davis, G., Messner, H., Umbreit, M.S. and Coates, R. (1992), *Making Amends: Mediation and Reparation in Criminal Justice,* Routledge, London and New York.

Department of Health (DoH) (1989), *The Care of Children: Principles and Practice in Regulations and Guidance,* HMSO, London.

Department of Health (DoH) (1991), *Volumes of Regulations and Guidance,* HMSO, London.

Department of Health (DoH) (1995a), *Child Protection: Messages from Research,* HMSO, London.

Department of Health (DoH) (1995b), *The Challenge of Partnership in Child Protection: A Guide for Practitioners,* HMSO, London.

Department of Health and Social Security (DHSS) (1985), *Social Work Decisions in Child Care*, HMSO, London.

Department of Social Welfare (1992), *Review of the Children Young Persons and Their Families Act 1989: Report of the Ministerial Review Team to the Minister of Social Welfare* (known as the *Mason Report*), Department of Social Welfare, Wellington.

Farmer, E. and Owen, M. (1995), *Child Protection Practice: Private Risks and Public Remedies - Decision-making, Intervention and Outcome in Child Protection Work*, HMSO, London.

Fisher, M., Marsh, P. and Phillips, D. (1986), *In and Out of Care: The Experiences of Children, Their Parents and Social Workers*, Batsford\BAAF, London.

Geddis, D.C. (1979), *Child Abuse: Report of a National Symposium held in Dunedin*, September 1979, National Children's Health Research Foundation, Dunedin.

Gibbons, J., Conroy, S. and Ball, C. (1995), *Operating the Child Protection System*, HMSO, London.

Hassall, I. and Maxwell, G. (1991), *The Family Group Conference: A Report from the Office of the Commissioner for Children*, Department of Social Welfare, Wellington.

Hassall, I. (1996), 'Origins and Development of Family Group Conferences', in J. Hudson, A. Morris, G. Maxwell and B. Galaway (eds), *Family Group Conferences: Perspectives on Policy and Practice*, The Federation Press, Annandale, NSW.

Hill, M. and Aldgate, J. (1996), *Child Welfare Services: Developments in Law, Policy, Practice and Research*,, Jessica Kingsley, London.

Holman, R. (1988), *Putting Families First*, Macmillan, London.

Home Office (1997), *Tackling Youth Crime: A Consultation Paper*, Home Office, London.

Home Office, Department of Health, Department of Education and Science, and Welsh Office (1991), *Working Together under the Children Act 1989: A Guide to Arrangements for Interagency Working for the Protection of Children from Abuse*, HMSO, London.

Jackson, S.E. (1998), 'Family Group Conferencing in Youth Justice: Issues for Implementation in England and Wales', *The Howard Journal of Criminal Justice*, vol. 37, no.1, pp. 34-51.

Kirkwood, A. (1992), *The Leicestershire Inquiry 1992*, Leicestershire County Council, Leicester.

Levy, A. and Kahan, B. (1991), *The Pindown Experience and the Protection of Children*, Staffordshire County Council, Stafford.

Lilja, J. (1997), *The Family Group Conference Project in Sweden*, Unpublished paper presented at the International Forum on Family Group Conferences, Winchester, 2-4 June, 1997.

Little, M. (1993), 'Specialist Residential Services for Difficult Adolescents: Some Recent Research Findings', in R. Bullock (ed), *Problem Adolescents,* Whiting and Birch, London.

Lupton, C. and Stevens, M. (1997), *Family Outcomes: Following through on Family Group Conferences,* Report No. 34, Social Services Research and Information Unit (SSRIU), University of Portsmouth.

Lupton, C., Barnard, S. and Swall-Yarrington, S. (1995), *Family Planning? An Evaluation of the Family Group Conference Model,* SSRIU, Portsmouth University.

Maxwell, G.M. and Morris, A. (1992), 'The Family Group Conference: A New Paradigm for Making Decisions about Children and Young People', *Children Australia,* vol. 17, pp. 11-15.

Maxwell, G.M. and Morris, A. (1993), *Families, Victims and Culture: Youth Justice in New Zealand,* Social Policy Agency and Institute of Criminology, Wellington.

McElrea, Judge F.W.M. (1995), *Accountability in the Community: Taking Responsibility for Offending,* A paper prepared for the Legal Research Foundation Conference, Auckland.

McKay, R.A. (1981), *Children in Foster Care - An Examination of the Case Histories of a Sample of Children in Care with Particular Emphasis on Placement of Children in Foster Homes,* Department of Social Welfare, Wellington.

Millham, S., Bullock, R., Hosie, K. and Little, M. (1986), *Lost in Care: The Problem of Maintaining Links between Children in Care and their Families,* Gower, Aldershot.

Millham, S., Bullock, R., Hosie, K. and Little, M. (1989), *Access Disputes in Child Care,* Gower, Aldershot.

Ministerial Advisory Committee (1986), *Puao-Te-Ata-Tu: The Report of the Ministerial Advisory Committee on a Maori Perspective for the Department of Social Welfare,* Department of Social Welfare, Wellington.

Mittler, H. (1992), 'Crossing Frontiers', *Community Care,* 12 November 1992, pp. 22-3.

Moore, D. (1995), *A New Approach to Juvenile Justice: An Evaluation of Family Group Conferencing in Wagga Wagga,* Centre for Rural Social Research, Wagga Wagga, NSW.

Morris, K. (1994), 'Family Group Conferences in the UK', in J Tunnard (ed) *Family Group Conferences: A Report Commissioned by the Department of Health,* Family Rights Group, London.

Morris, K., Marsh, P. and Wiffen, J. (1998), *A Training Pack for Family Group Conferences,* Family Rights Group, London.

National Children's and Youth Law Centre (1995), *Rights Now!,* vol. 3, no. 4, University of New South Wales, pp. 1-3.

Nixon, P. (1992), *Family Group Conferences: A Radical Approach to Planning the Care and Protection of Children,* Unpublished paper, Hampshire County Council, Winchester.

Office for National Statistics (1997), *Social Focus on Families,* HMSO, London.

Packman, J., Randall, J., and Jacques, N. (1986), *Who Needs Care? Social Work Decisions about Children,* Blackwell, London.

Packman, J. (1993), 'From Prevention to Partnership: Child Welfare Services across Three Decades', in Pugh, G. (ed), *Thirty Years of Change for Children,* National Children's Bureau, London.

Parton, N. (1991), *Governing the Family,* Macmillan, London.

Paterson, K. and Harvey, M. (1991), *Organisation and Operation of Care and Protection Family Group Conferences,* Evaluation Unit, Department of Social Welfare, Wellington.

Pennell, J. and Burford, G. (1994), 'Widening the Circle: Family Group Decision-making', *Journal of Child and Youth Care,* vol. 9, pp. 1-11.

Pennell, J. and Burford, G. (1997), 'Addressing Domestic Violence through Family Group Decision-making', Unpublished paper presented at the International Forum on FGCs, 2-4 June, Winchester.

Pilalis J., Tanieulu Rev. M. and Opai, S. (1988), *Dangerous Situations,* Department of Social Welfare, Wellington.

Renouf, J., Robb, G. and Walls. P. (1990), *Children, Young Persons and their Families Act 1989: Report of the First Year of Operation,* Department of Social Welfare, Wellington.

Rowe, J., Cain, H., Hundleby, M. and Keane, A. (1984), *Long Term Foster Care,* Batsford/BAAF, London.

Rowe, J., Hundleby, M. and Garnett, L. (1989), *Child Care Now: A Survey of Child Care Patterns,* BAAF Research Series 6, London.

Ryan, M. (1993), *The Children Act 1989: Putting it into Practice,* Arena, Aldershot.

Ryburn, M. (1992), 'Family Group Conferences', in J. Thoburn (ed) *Practice in Participation: Involving Families in Child Protection,* HMSO, London.

Ryburn, M. (1994a), 'Planning for Children Here and in New Zealand: A Comparison of the Legislation', in J. Tunnard (ed). *Family Group Conferences: A Report Commissioned by the Department of Health,* Family Rights Group, London.

Ryburn, M. (1994b), 'Contact after Contested Adoptions', *Adoption and Fostering,* vol. 18, pp. 30-8.

Ryburn, M. and Atherton, C. (1996), 'Family Group Conferences: Partnership in Practice', *Adoption and Fostering,* vol. 20, pp.16-23.

Schmidt, B.D. (1978), *Child Protection Team Handbook,* STPM Press, New York.

Shapland, J., Willmore, J. and Duff, P. (1985), *Victims in the Criminal Justice System,* Gower, Aldershot.

145

Sinclair, R., Garnett, L. and Berridge, D. (1995), *Social Work and Assessment with Adolescents,* National Children's Bureau, London.

Tapp, P.F. (1990), 'Family Group Conferences and the Children, Young Persons and their Families Act 1989: An Ineffective Statute?', *New Zealand Recent Law Review,* pp. 82-88.

Thoburn, J., Lewis, A. and Shemmings, D. (1995), *Paternalism or Partnership? Family Involvement in the Child Protection Process,* HMSO, London.

Thornton, C. (1993), *Family Group Conferences: A Literature Review,* Practitioners Publishing, Lower Hutt.

Von Dadelzen, J. (1987), *Sexual Abuse Study, An Examination of the Histories of Sexual Abuse among Girls Currently in the Care of the Department of Social Welfare,* Department of Social Welfare, Wellington.

Walgrave, L. (1995), 'Restorative Justice for Juveniles: Just a Technique or a Fully Fledged Alternative?', *The Howard Journal,* vol. 34, pp. 228-249.

Wedge, P. and Mantle, G. (1991), *Sibling Groups and Social Work: A Study of Children Released for Permanent Family Placement,* Avebury, Aldershot.

Wilcox, R., Smith, D., Moore, J., Hewitt, A., Allan, G., Walker, H., Ropatu, M., Monu, L. and Featherstone, T. (1991), *Family Decision-making: Family Group Conferences, Practitioners Views,* Practitioners Publishing, Lower Hutt.

Wright, M. (1991), *Justice for Victims and Offenders,* Open University Press, Milton Keynes.

Wright, M. (1995), 'Victims, Mediation and Criminal Justice', *Criminal Law Review,* pp. 187-99.

7 Family Group Conferences: A Co-ordinator's Perspective

MARILYN TAYLOR

When I was in care we had case conferences. We knew they were going on but couldn't go. Then we could go and all these people I hardly knew, knew all these things about me - I'd ball my eyes out. I would wonder what they were talking about as I was waiting to go in.
(Young person)

It's (Family Group Conferences) a reasonable method. At least you can air views and make a contribution. In the past, professionals have made a decision and you don't feel it's the right one. The family can make a better decision because they have the larger picture.
(Young person)

It was like a wedding reception. You knew there were going to be people there you didn't like but it was important to go.
(Family member)

All the above quotations are from Lupton et al, (1995), *Family Planning? An Evaluation of the Family Conference Model.*

Introduction

Children's experiences of the traditional care system have been far from positive. Family Group Conferences (FCGs) have been posited as a way of rectifying this situation. In this paper, I will look at Family Group Conferences as a way of enabling families to be directly involved and responsible for decisions made about their children and young people. I will also consider the concept of empowerment as embedded in this way of working, and discuss the differential impact of this on various players in the model. Additionally, I will examine how the co-ordinator can act as a broker in the relationship between statutory authority and family, and facilitate the implementation of a partnership between the different parties.

The writer's particular experience in England is as a co-ordinator in the Hampshire Project, as a trainer of professionals, and more recently as a manager of the model in Southampton. This paper will draw on knowledge gained through these roles, and also by reference to the wider national and international situations. The voices of children, young people and their families will be expressed through the use of case material. This has been sufficiently disguised to ensure confidentiality, whilst preserving the essence of the issues raised.

I have found that working as a co-ordinator for Family Group Conferences has been one of the most exciting pieces of work with which I have been engaged in a professional social work career spanning three decades. The underlying philosophy of properly informing, respecting and empowering families is one that sits easily with my other role as a social work manager in a voluntary organisation working with families. Very rarely as a social worker does one experience a 'buzz' as families who are used to feeling only failure and inadequacy find that despite the difficulties and pain of a Conference, they can make a good plan for their child that is at least equal to anything that a meeting of professionals can achieve. To enable a process whereby families can experience such a sense of profound achievement by acting together for their child is a privilege and a pleasure. But this process is not without dilemmas and problems.

The Co-ordinator's Role

The explanation of the Family Group Conference model is relatively simple and straightforward. But the simplicity of the model can disguise the complexity of the dilemmas it exposes, not least with respect to professionals, and the attitudes and beliefs about families that inform their work. I shall refer to the co-ordinator as 'she' throughout, not for any gender bias, but for simplicity of writing. For similar reasons, the social worker will be referred to as 'he'.

The co-ordinator receives a referral from the project manager. She normally discusses this first with the referrer, who is usually the family social worker. She listens to the concerns raised by the social worker, and identifies the key questions to be answered. She tries hard to remain neutral and not take on any agendas or opinions about the family that the professional might share. She then makes contact with the family, usually starting with the key parent or parents and the child or young person. She works with them to identify all the people who are, or who have been, of significance to the child. 'Significant people' can also include anyone outside the family, such as friends or neighbours, who have been important to the child. She then makes contact with all these people, usually involving a visit, if at all possible.

She explains to all the members of the family the process of a Family Group Conference and invites them to the meeting. She arranges the meeting venue, in a place and at a time that the family chooses. This can be open to negotiation, as it is important that key professionals who have crucial information to give to the family in order for them to reach their decision are able to attend. Nonetheless, the family has the final say as to when this meeting should take place. Often this is a weekday afternoon or evening, but weekend meetings are not unknown. It is helpful if everyone concerned is reasonably flexible and adaptable.

She also arranges the meal. This is seen as important for a number of reasons. It can act as an icebreaker if things are tense. It has symbolic significance on family occasions of importance. And, it is tangible evidence of the importance that is given to this event. Again, the family decide how this meal should be organised and of what it should consist.

It is helpful that when members of the meeting arrive they are greeted with tea or coffee and biscuits. The meal itself can take place at this stage, if the family wishes. But often, family members are too tense to want to eat much at this early stage. More substantial food disappears faster when the professionals have left, or at the end of the whole process.

The meeting itself takes place in three stages. The co-ordinator chairs the first stage. The family are welcomed and invited to introduce themselves according to their relationship to the child or young person whose Conference it is. It is helpful to remind the family that everyone is at the meeting because of their importance to the child or young person in their family. This reminder ensures that the meeting is child focused, and acts against previous enmities and conflicts that can otherwise dominate the process.

The family is reminded of the reason for the meeting and the key questions to be addressed. It is helpful if these are written on a sheet of flip chart paper and hung somewhere where everyone can see them clearly. It is also best if these questions are kept brief and very focused. For instance, 'Where should Karen live?' or 'How can Karen be kept safe?'

The co-ordinator revisits any ground rules, such as practising respect for all members of the meeting and expressing disagreement without threatening the others present. The co-ordinator then asks the professionals in turn to share their concerns with respect to the questions to be answered, focusing on the present situation, and looking towards future plans, rather than revisiting old history. The family is encouraged to ask questions of fact or clarification. The professionals are also asked to log up any resources that their departments may have to offer to the situation. Sometimes, professionals worry that this will mean that families will ask for expensive resources involving large investment on the part of the agencies. In practice this is rare: families are much more likely to produce a plan that is wide ranging and includes a reliance on family resources.

When the family feels it has enough information, the co-ordinator asks the professionals to withdraw. This can be a tricky moment for some professionals who can be seduced by requests to linger. But it is an absolute imperative for the FGC model that there is a second stage of private family time with no professionals present. The role of the co-ordinator is to ensure that the professionals do leave, and they may need a little encouragement to do so! The co-ordinator then checks out with the family that it is clear about its role, that is, to produce a plan that makes decisions in response to the concerns raised. The co-ordinator will then also leave, but will make clear that she will be nearby, and available for help with process issues if things become difficult. For instance, if the family gets stuck, the co-ordinator may suggest taking a break, or dividing into smaller groups for a while. But the co-ordinator will be clear that it is not her role to suggest the content of the plan.

During the second stage, the role of the co-ordinator is to wait outside, but to be sensitive to anyone leaving the meeting, and respond to distress or concerns. From waiting outside a number of FGCs, it is apparent from the noise that they can sometimes go through a difficult 'storming' phase when anger is expressed and feelings generally ventilated. This can be a nerve wracking time for the co-ordinator in an adjoining room, and to the social worker who has remained too. The co-ordinator may have a role to reassure a social worker inexperienced with FGCs that intervention would not be helpful. But as a co-ordinator it is very supportive to have a colleague who can help with working with any members of the Conference who walk out and need someone to give them time and to help them go back and re-engage with the decision-making process.

But after the anger has been shared, the questions remain to be answered and it feels from the outside that the meeting goes through a more focused stage. The time outside varies, but on average is about an hour. A member of the family will ask the co-ordinator to return. Sometimes, the plan is already written clearly on the flip chart, and there is nothing much more to do other than to help the family share it with the social worker and receive some immediate feedback as to whether or not it is acceptable to social services. At other times, the family may have made some clear decisions, but be unsure how to express them. The co-ordinator will then help them to do this, but in their own words. There may be a sensitive role to accomplish in helping the family to be specific and time-focused without interfering in the essentials of the plan. For instance, if an aunt is offering 'to have David to stay sometimes', it can be helpful to encourage this to be more definite as to when and how it may take place.

The co-ordinator will also check out the monitoring and reviewing arrangements for the plan, and may ask the family to think more clearly about how and when they want this done, and who they want to take responsibility for this task to be achieved.

The remaining task for the co-ordinator is to thank the family for the work they have done, and recognise the achievements that this represents. Often, the family members can be feeling very pleased with themselves by this stage. Seemingly insuperable problems of bringing warring parties together have been overcome, and the family has focused on the crucial issues concerning the child, and produced an innovative and creative plan to address them.

The co-ordinator will ensure that all members of the Conference receive a copy of the family plan. The co-ordinator's role is then to withdraw from the process, and leave the family and the professionals to get on with the task of implementing the plan. However, experience is showing that this total withdrawal may need to be looked at again.

Research has indicated that although the process of Family Group Conferences are overwhelmingly seen as positive by participants, attitudes towards outcomes and the implementation of all items on the plan is less positive (Lupton and Stevens, 1997). There may be a further task for co-ordinators being involved in the reviewing process.

What Makes a Good Co-ordinator?

Much has been said above about the role of the co-ordinator being pivotal in the FGC process. It is vital to recruit the right person for the job. But what sort of mix of skills, knowledge and experience are we seeking? Is a professional social worker the obvious choice to make? The question presents a dilemma which different projects have resolved in various ways.

In Hampshire, the group of co-ordinators contains social workers who have retired or are wanting to work fewer hours in order to spend more time with their small children. The group also contains social work educators, professional counsellors, nurses, community workers, ex-education welfare officers, probation officers and social workers in the voluntary sector. Colleagues from New Zealand are almost always social workers. But the possibilities are wider than this. Co-ordinators in Sweden, for instance, come from a much wider mix, including social workers, but also people whose previous jobs could be roofing or taxi driving!

Having a wide range of people involved seemed to those in the Hampshire Project to provide a very rich pool of possibilities, and was nearer to a concept of identifying key people in the community who have status and trust for their personal rather than their professional qualities. These essential personal characteristics might include the following:

- imagination and creativity - to suggest different ways of resolving dilemmas and problems when families or professionals become 'stuck' and need help in moving onto the next stage;
- flexibility - to work in new ways that empower children, young people and their families, to have an ability to 'think on one's feet', and be open to different methods and solutions;
- commitment to empowerment - an understanding of the implications and complexities that this involves;

- sensitivity to diversity - to value and enjoy the wide cultural variety in which families operate, and to ensure that this informs the way in which a Conference is managed;
- respect - to be committed to enabling a Conference to take place that gives equality of respect to all parties - family, friends and professionals, as expressed, for instance, by the terms of address;
- tenacity and determination - to set up a Conference in the face of a multitude of obstacles and difficulties that can emanate from people who may be fearful or suspicious of the implications of an FGC;
- independence - to have the motivation to operate on one's own in an environment that can sometimes feel hostile and lonely, and to do so without giving in to the temptation to cut corners. This is particularly pertinent in the initial stage of making contact with people, inviting them to the Conference, and ensuring that they are well-prepared;
- energy - to do all the above well and with enthusiasm;
- last, but perhaps not least, a dogged belief in the capacity of a Family Group Conference to release the potential of the wider kinship group to achieve a good plan for their child or young person. This is a quality that helps a co-ordinator to battle through the many problems and contrary indications that can be a feature of the preparatory period, and inspire others with the confidence to do the same.

Such paragons of virtue and competence also need skills of communication, negotiation, mediation, facilitation, organisation and administration! It can be argued that the role of an FGC co-ordinator demands skills and personal qualities of a very high standard. But, it might also be supposed that a group of co-ordinators with such a breadth and depth of skill and knowledge might be more readily recruited from a potential market that is not limited to a few more obvious professionals.

The Independence of the Co-ordinator

The co-ordinator has a degree of independence as she is not an employee of the Social Services Department, but works on a sessional basis. She is paid to set up this Family Group Conference with the family, but to have no agenda for its outcome. She can negotiate arrangements for when and where it will happen between the family and the professionals, remembering all the time that it should be at a place and time of the family's choosing. Simultaneously, she must hold onto the restraints of the realities of when key professionals are able and willing to attend. Without specific pieces of information, the family's task of making the best plan will be hampered. Although most FGCs are held in the afternoon or evening, it is not unknown for the family to insist on a weekend. The professionals need to be helped to be flexible, but the family also needs to be aware of the other professional and personal demands on people's lives.

The Co-ordinator's Support Group

An essential tool for the co-ordinator is access to regular meetings of a support group of peers. It is here that current issues can be raised and problems shared. The work feels so new, and relatively unexplored that such a forum has a special pertinence and importance. The role of co-ordinator can be experienced as both a science and an art. There are specific responsibilities and boundaries. The range of skills, knowledge and attitudes has already been discussed above. But there is also an intangible personal style and individual perspective that a co-ordinator brings to the job that it is helpful to share and explore with others involved in the same work. A forum of the co-ordinators' support group, together with access to individual supervision, ensures that the work is both well supported and is accountable. It also enables the voice of the co-ordinator to be heard in the development of the local Family Group Conference scheme.

The Relationship between the Co-ordinator and the Referrer

The relationship between the co-ordinator and the referrer is a key one. Its nature can be crucial to the process of setting up the Family Group Conferences, the meeting itself, and to the success of implementing the outcome of the plan. Making a referral for a Family Group Conference is not the time for a social worker to go on annual leave! Doing so can be interpreted as someone wanting to ensure that a family in crisis has some other professional actively involved during his or her absence. Less generously, it might be seen as a device to undermine the success of the Conference which is bringing in a new and resented way of working with families that is being actively promoted by management.

Once the process of planning for a Conference begins, sometimes from the initial idea of a possible referral discussed with the family by the social worker, and almost always from the first meeting of the co-ordinator with the family, telephones begin to ring and contacts within the family are made or re-established. Issues that require a social worker's input can quickly rise to the surface. These can be problems that have taken a secondary role until now, but have assumed a higher prominence with the anticipation of an FGC. Almost certainly, things will have to be clarified, and information gathered to be shared at a Conference.

Some vulnerable members of the family may need special support in preparing for a Conference, which they find unnerving. Handling such situations needs the co-operation of both the social worker and co-ordinator. Two cases serve to illustrate the impact of this crucial relationship, one where it was difficult to establish because of the absence of the social worker during the preparatory period, and the second where the success of a very difficult referral was substantially improved because of a very close and positive working relationship between the social worker and co-ordinator.

Case Study No 1 - An Absent Social Worker

A small baby, Ann, was referred for a Family Group Conference. She was only a few weeks old, and the child of a 15 year old mother. There was confusion about future planning for this child. Initially, the mother had requested adoption, but now was not so sure. The maternal grandmother and other members of the mother's family did not want the child adopted. They had tried to resolve the problem themselves. The mother's older brother and sister-in-law had attempted to look after Ann, but this had not been successful. There were too many pressures on them from their own small children. So, Ann had returned to her mother. The expectation from the referral was that adoption outside the family would be the natural and best outcome from the FGC.

From the time that the co-ordinator first made contact with the family, many problems became apparent. The young mother was withdrawn, staying much of the time by herself in the bedroom. She had been out of school for several months, and had lost contact with her peers. Plans for her own education seemed hazy and unclear. In the opinion of the co-ordinator, this young woman was deeply depressed. She seemed in no state to make crucial decisions about the future of her baby whilst her own needs were so substantially neglected. At fifteen, she was only a child herself. It seemed imperative that the FGC address the needs of the mother before considering those of her baby: they were so entwined.

A number of issues needed to be addressed in this important preparatory stage of the FGC. For instance, a referral to the appropriate psychiatric service for the mother. Information needed to be gathered about the educational services available to the mother, and what professional support might be available to her.

But for the major part of this period, the social worker was away on holiday. The co-ordinator found herself breaking the boundaries of work that were inappropriate for her very specific role, and was making contacts with professionals that could be seen to be properly the responsibility of the social worker. The close relationship that needed to be established between these two people during this stage was unable to happen in the absence of the social worker, so that the meeting with the family took place with this vacuum still operating.

Case Study No 2 - Co-ordinator and Social Worker Co-operate

Jane was a widow with two daughters, Sarah aged 11 and Katy aged 9. She had become severely depressed since the suicide of her husband two years earlier. There had been marital difficulties before the suicide, and her husband David, had left a note blaming her for his death. David's side of the family had held her responsible for the tragedy, and had not kept in contact since the inquest.

Over recent months Jane's depression had deepened and she had been admitted to hospital for some weeks. This had happened quite suddenly, and the girls had been taken into the care of the local authority without much planning or preparation. They had been placed in a foster home, where they were both angry and unhappy. They felt strongly that this should not have happened, and that someone in their family should have offered them a temporary home.

By the time of the referral for a Family Group Conference, the girls were back home. But Jane was still ill, and a further hospital admittance was anticipated. Sarah and Katy wanted something different to happen next time. An FGC was discussed with them by their social workers. They all felt anxious but positive about the idea. Jane was very nervous about the prospect of meeting and again facing her husband's hostile and accusing relatives, even though she was aware that they may be source of some support and help.

The FGC was arranged in a record time of only five working days, not only because of the urgency of the situation, but also in recognition that Jane's anxiety could not be contained for much longer. The anticipation of this confrontation could be seen as increasing the risks arising out of Jane's own mental illness.

The active involvement and close working relationship between the social worker and the co-ordinator was crucial during this difficult time of preparation for the FGC. The social worker was making daily visits to Jane and spending considerable time with her. She listened to her fears and supported her courage in taking some personal risk by being open to this meeting. Much credit was given to Jane's willingness to go ahead with something that seemed to offer the prospect of positive outcomes for her daughters but at some cost to herself.

The co-ordinator also was visiting daily, involving all the family in the preparation and planning for the meeting and supporting them through their fears. The co-ordinator was also making contact with David's side of the family. They had not known that the girls had been in a foster home, and were now feeling much more positive and supportive of Jane. This was fed back to Jane by the co-ordinator.

By working together, sharing on a daily basis the current level of Jane's anxieties and the attitudes of the wider family, the co-ordinator and social worker were able to sustain Jane during a very difficult time before the meeting took place. Had this not worked so well, the risk factors in this stage of the FGC process would have been substantially higher. The eventual outcome of the meeting was a detailed and sensitive plan for the two children, and a warm reconciliation between the two sides of the family. Jane came away from the Conference feeling supported by the wider family in a way that could not have been envisaged previously.

The Co-ordinator as Broker of Relationships between Family and Agencies

Working with families in a state of crisis is a task fraught with possibilities for misunderstandings and for the projection of negative feelings. If superimposed onto this is a shortage of agency resources to help directly, and a situation of overworked and over-stressed staff, then the risks are magnified. The co-ordinator can come into a situation where the family has been frustrated, disappointed and disillusioned with the social services department, and the agency has labelled the family as hostile and difficult. A referral for an FGC can be seen as a means of making a problematic and dependent family face realities, and be forced to take responsibility for itself. It is possible that such a motive can have punitive undertones. Alternatively, it can be seen as trying a new method where all else has failed.

The independence of the co-ordinator then becomes of particular significance in this context. It is especially important that the co-ordinator present herself as neutral, with the role of a facilitator charged with the task of enabling a certain process to take place. Her role is quite discreet. It has a clear beginning, a middle and an end in a process that is time limited. This independence and clearly defined role can assist her acting as a broker or a bridge in the relationship between a family and the social services department. She can put flesh on the concept of partnership between the social services department and families, an injunction which is fundamental to the spirit of the 1989 Children Act. The co-ordinator brings no bagage to the relationship from previous knowledge of the history of the family or the agency's work with them. As her role is time limited and specific, there should be no room for a personal involvement in the outcome of the meeting.

It is important that the co-ordinator has highly developed skills of negotiation. She must be able to listen sensitively to concerns and fears raised by both the family and by the professionals. People who have encountered problems in their relationships can fear the exposure and confrontation that can be a feature particularly of the first stage of the meeting. Social workers and social work teams that are new to FGC can be helped by a co-ordinator who is skilled and willing to support and nurture them through a new and perceived 'risky' way of working. Much is said

158

about the social worker losing 'power' in the FGC process. But this can be reframed in terms of the Family Group Conference process demanding a shift in the sort of skills being required of the social worker and other professionals. These can be defined as facilitating skills, which are arguably of a higher level than those requiring direct action. A good co-ordinator can help the social worker to prepare for his part in the FGC, and refine his facilitating and enabling skills.

Families may have felt that the services so far offered by the agency have been shoddy and unsatisfactory. If the pressures of work have meant a reduced level of service, then this may need recognising and acknowledging in order for the process to continue.

Case Study No 3 - Negotiating Complex Situations

As the co-ordinator, Amy felt that initially she was not accepted by either the Social Services Department or by the family. There was a history of ambivalence and animosity between the two parties. The Social Services Department felt that this apparently affluent and middle-class family should have been able to work out the solution to their family's dilemma without using up the scarce resources of their own agency. The family, perhaps because of their cultural background, had high expectations of the nature of a professional relationship, what services a client might expect, and how it might be delivered. They felt that social services had been greatly lacking both in the quality of what had been offered in the past, and in the nature of its delivery.

The family was struggling with providing care for Kathy, the fourteen year old daughter of a divorced mother with significant mental health problems, who had been in and out of psychiatric hospital for some time. The recent profound reduction in the mother's financial situation, meant that private health care was no longer accessible, and further exacerbated this situation. There were a number of relatives and friends involved, but most were living some distance from the family, and had busy professional lives. The central and key support in the situation came from a school teacher at the independent school which Kathy still attended.

The social work team from which this referral came was very new to using FGCs in their work. Amy felt that this referral might be seen as a way of ensuring that the wider kinship network provided all the solutions to the dilemmas posed by Kathy's predicament, and that the department could hope to close the case as a result of the FGC. The family acted in a way that showed they believed nothing good was likely to come from anything that the Social Services Department suggested, and was initially hostile and suspicious of the co-ordinator.

Amy felt that her first task as co-ordinator was to get alongside the social worker and her team. Achieving this objective required a substantial amount of work. Amy approached this task with a clear view of both her own role in the FGC process, and also that of the social worker. This early stage made demands on the skills of the co-ordinator both as facilitator and as educator, enabling the social worker to understand the potential of the FGC, and the demands that it might make on her own time and skills.

Amy was an experienced co-ordinator. But she found that working with this family was especially difficult in terms of enabling its members, particularly the mother and Kathy's older siblings, to accept her role. One of these siblings had provided care for Kathy when their mother was in hospital and responded more readily to Amy's initiatives. But the other brother and sister were more difficult to engage. Their lives were too 'busy' to make time for a meeting emanating from Social Services.

After a number of meetings with both the family and the professionals involved, the co-ordinator felt that dead-lock had been reached, and that there was no motivation for a Conference to take place. Amy was feeling that she had failed to engage the family, including the young person who was at the centre of the process.

Two key factors reversed this impression. The first and most crucial of these was a second meeting with Kathy. She was now certain that she wanted an FGC to take place. This provided the driving force to ensure that it would happen. It also reinforced the importance of working hard at this relationship in the preparatory stages of the FGC. The second was the encouragement given by other key people in the scenario, particularly the school teacher, who had acted in a pivotal role during times when Kathy's mother was hospitalised.

The co-ordinator worked hard to bring other key players into the Conference, especially those in the psychiatric field. This not only ensured that the family would have access to the crucial information needed to make optimal use of this opportunity for decision-making, but also served to take the weight off the social worker and the Social Services

Department, who were likely to receive some criticism. Amy worked hard with the social worker to prepare for the potentially difficult first stage of the meeting and to share how as the co-ordinator and Chair, she would handle problems that might arise during this stage.

Amy gave the mother considerable time to talk and communicate her anxieties and her frustrations, receiving and replying to masses of lengthy letters and faxes in a way that indicated that she was being heard. A gentle humour was also used by the co-ordinator to disarm some of the tensions in the situation, particularly at the beginning of the Conference when family and professionals were gathering for the meeting.

The outcome of the meeting was a plan that addressed the needs of Kathy should her mother need hospitalisation, and included a new network of support from family, friends and professionals.

The Cultural Sensitivity of the Model, and the Impact of the Co-ordinator

The FGC concept originated in New Zealand from the Maori traditional ways of resolving problems. The ideas governing its development were outlined in a Report from the Ministerial Advisory Commission for Maori Social Welfare called *Puao-Te-Ata-Tu*, meaning 'daybreak' or 'dawn'. This made suggestions for the state to work in a more culturally-sensitive way with Maori young people who were caught up in the family and child welfare system or in the youth justice system. The concept of FGCs were enshrined in New Zealand's Children, Young Persons and their Families Act, 1989. This was enacted in the same year as the Children Act for England and Wales, which addressed similar concerns. It is an example of an idea originating from a minority culture, but whose seeds are beginning to grow in various parts of the globe. The FGC represents a challenging reversal of the more usual imposition of Western white culture on ethnic minority ones. But perhaps the model of a large kinship network coming together to share information, consult together and propose solutions to problems goes back to the early roots of all our cultures. We may just be experiencing a re-discovery of a simple and natural way of family decision-making that have been used over the millennia, but lost during the last century of Western industrial development.

Crow and Marsh (1997) outline the five key features of the FGC model as follows:

- an independent co-ordinator;
- a wide and inclusive notion of the extended family;
- information giving in plain and concise ways;
- the private family time;
- a process of negotiating and agreeing the plan.

These characteristics are what define this method as different from other decision-making processes and ways of involving the family in them. But within these constraints the family is able to make key decisions about how the process happens. The meeting is normally in the first language of the family. The meal provided will reflect cultural norms, as will the manner in which the particular Conference is conducted. Morris and Tunnard (1996) refer to a range of FGCs throughout the world, all of which reflect the particular patterns of local culture.

Cultural-sensitivity and anti-discriminatory practice raise particular issues for FGCs and the role of the co-ordinator. It is important that the recruitment and selection of a group of co-ordinators reflects the ethnic make-up of the local population. Black co-ordinators do not always want to be identified to work with black families, but it is important that there is a rich cultural diversity of knowledge and experience available to the development of the local model. It is also important that co-ordinators have access to the skills and knowledge of relevant cultural consultants, as it is very easy to make assumptions about the way in which families operate, and effortlessly stampede through cultural norms and sensitivities.

A New Zealand colleague describes the Samoan norm that the lead person in a meeting, such as that assumed by the co-ordinator in a FGC meeting, will always sit at a higher level to the assembled group. Therefore, if the Chair of the Conference slumps casually low in her seat, she will find that the other participants in the meeting are sinking lower and lower towards the floor! Most cultures are shot through with rules around food and eating that are painfully easy to break without previous warning or knowledge.

The FGC Projects in Hampshire and in Southampton, which are best known to the writer, are still struggling with recruiting a representative number of black and Asian co-ordinators, and with promoting referrals from black families (see Lupton and Stevens, 1997). It seems that little is known about the reasons for the latter, but we need more specific research about this feature of the Projects, and their greater promotion amongst social workers and managers.

The Differential Empowerment of the Family

The concept of power that is distributed between professionals and family members is complex and challenging. The quotations from young people and family members at the beginning of this chapter refer positively to the shift of power from professionals to the family that the FGC model represents. This is a real experience in Conferences, and research reflects the substantially positive feedback from family members as a result (Lupton et al, 1995; Lupton and Stevens, 1997).

For family members who have experienced professionals coming into their lives and making decisions for them that they see as damaging, this alternative way of working can be difficult to take on board initially. There is sometimes a moment when as a co-ordinator it is possible to perceive the light of belief gleam in someone's eyes. For one of the young people in Case Study No 1 above, this occurred when the co-ordinator asked what food the girls would like at their Conference. The reply was that they wanted sandwiches. It was when the co-ordinator asked what sort of sandwiches, and duly wrote down their response, that their eyes seemed to say that this woman really meant what she was saying!

Another co-ordinator also experienced two young children taking over their Conference in a very direct way. She turned back from helping members of the meeting to tea and biscuits to find that the sheet of flip chart paper on which she had written a 'Welcome to Sally and Daniel's Family Group Conference' message was now fully illustrated with cartoon drawings of all the family members that were gathering together!

But sometimes the empowerment offered or experienced is not so straightforward. In a family engaged in internal conflict, the empowerment of one individual can be seen as the disempowerment of others. In these situations, power can be experienced as a finite entity, rather than something that can be generally enlarged. Then there are complexities or implications for other family members, other professionals or the process itself.

Case Study No 4 - Empowering Families is a Difficult Process

Helen was a young single mother with a three year old son. She was struggling with the care of her child, and the social worker had concerns. She was on bail for an offence of assault, and the case was coming to court imminently. It was likely that she would receive a prison sentence. Decisions had to be reached about the support that was necessary to sustain Helen's care of her son generally, and also about his care should she go to prison. Someone had to make these decisions. If it was not through a Family Group Conference, then it would be done by the professionals. If the matter was decided after Helen had been sentenced, and therefore, not around, her involvement in any decision taken would be substantially reduced.

Helen was initially ambivalent about a FGC. She was reluctant to involve her family, and that of the child's father. They were of an older generation, and in her view, were interfering and critical. Nevertheless, she agreed to go ahead with the Conference. The rest of the family were enthusiastic, and some members went to considerable lengths to attend. For example, a grandparent came down from Scotland at her own expense in order to participate in what she considered to be an essential decision-making task for the family that needed everyone's support.

The evening before the Conference, Helen changed her mind about the meeting. She informed the co-ordinator that she wanted it cancelled, and that she would just tell her social worker what should happen if she were to be sent to prison. She was not be persuaded otherwise, and insisted on the cancellation of the Conference. A crucial resource in the armoury of a co-ordinator is ready access to supervision in which difficulties which arise can be considered. After consulting with her supervisor, the co-ordinator decided to go ahead anyway.

Helen, the mother, was not pleased! This was not her understanding of empowerment. Despite protests to the contrary, Helen did attend the Conference, but her anger with the co-ordinator was palpable! The co-ordinator dealt with Helen's anger, which seemed to reflect some fear that her own position as mother might be undermined by the rest of the

Conference, by both acknowledging an understanding of the anger, and by stressing Helen's powerful position as the only person with parental rights in the situation. Any decisions reached and plans made by the meeting would need Helen's approval. The mother rose to this recognition and support for her position, and everyone was pleased that the family had made sound decisions about their child, despite considerable personal difficulties and conflict.

Case Study 5 - Peer Empowerment

Although peer support for children is not generally pursued in FGCs, the following example indicates that it can operate in a positive manner.

Penny was a young person who had been in the care of the local authority for ten years. She was very damaged from the series of foster home breakdowns and poor relationships with her own family. After some very challenging behaviour she was now in secure accommodation to ensure her personal safety. But she would not be able to live here much longer, and alternative plans had to be made.

A number of people, mostly professionals and foster parents, had a stake in the outcome of this Conference. In fact, it seemed that because of a general disinterest in her expressed by her family, it was only those people who had been most involved in Penny's care over the last few years who would attend. But most had an opinion of Penny that would make it difficult for her to have a strong voice in the proceedings. There was a real problem about how to enable Penny to be empowered to have her own views listened to with meaning, and for her to experience it as such. Decisions about her life had always been made up to now by professionals.

Penny was adamant that the person she wanted to be at the Conference for her, as an 'advocate' at the meeting, was Tracey, another young woman who was living at her previous children's home. Tracey was equally perceived by most of the professionals as damaged, difficult and generally unsuitable for this role. But when the co-ordinator visited Tracey and explained the process and the role that her friend wanted her to play, she rose to the occasion and to the trust and responsibility demonstrated by the request. She needed some help herself from the co-ordinator to face a meeting perceived as being initiated by the Social Services Department. But she acted with dignity and competence on the occasion in a way that perhaps no adult professional could have managed with Penny. She was sensitive to her needs, and was able to take her out of the meeting for a break when tensions rose. She talked through with her how she should proceed, and to what she should agree. The eventual plan was deemed acceptable by all parties by the end of the evening.

This was also a case where close co-operation between an involved and sensitive social worker enabled the co-ordinator to achieve her task with a success that might otherwise have been difficult to obtain otherwise.

Conclusion

Family Group Conferences are developing in an increasing number of local authorities, and the implementation of the model is gaining momentum. Sometimes, this happens as a result of a decision by management, and there is a top-down approach. Sometimes, the knowledge and interest comes from specific practitioners who bring previous experience and enthusiasm to a new area, and act to inspire and motivate from a grassroots level. This was the experience in Hampshire.

Although the model can seem simple, its realisation is much more complex, and the issues it raises are diverse. Its underlying philosophy is one of empowerment and partnership. It feels important, therefore, that these principles are not lost in the implementation, and that co-ordinators and service users are able to have a voice in the development of any local project.

There is a need for accountability, equality of access to Family Group Conferences, and parity of the quality of service offered. However, in the rush to ensure that these important aspects are built into the plan for implementation, there may be a danger of over-structuring the service and thereby rob it of the very qualities that make it attractive to families, that is, its flexibility and responsiveness to individual needs. There has been some argument for distancing the management by contracting it out to the voluntary sector (Marsh and Crow, 1998). But in itself this does not necessarily prevent the service becoming bureaucratised, or losing its flexible approach. It is more important to ensure that certain critical criteria are met whatever the management arrangements. Perhaps the most crucial of these is that of the skilled and independent co-ordinator, who has a voice in the development of the local project, and is properly supported and valued.

References

Crow, G. and Marsh, P. (1997), *Family Group Conferences, Partnership and Child Welfare: A Research Report on Four Pilot Projects in England and Wales,,* University of Sheffield, Sheffield.
Crow, G. and Marsh, P. (1998), *Family Group Conferences in Child Welfare,* Blackwell, Oxford.
Department of Health (1995), *Child Protection: Messages from Research,* HMSO, London.
Hamill, H. (1996), *Family Group Conferences in Child Care Practice,* University of East Anglia Monographs, Norwich.
Hudson, J., Morris, A., Maxwell, G. and Galaway, B. (1996), *Family Group Conferences: Perspectives on Policy and Practice,* The Federation Press - Criminal Justice Press, London.
Lupton, C., Barnard, S., Swall-Yarrington, M. (1995), *Family Planning? An Evaluation of the Family Group Conference Model,* Social Services Research and Information Unit, Portsmouth.
Morris, K. (1995), *Family Group Conference: An Introductory Pack,* Family Rights Group, London.
Morris, K. and Tunnard, J. (1996), *Family Group Conferences: Messages from UK Practice and Research,* Family Rights Group, London.

8 Crossing Reality - Building Networks around Families in Crisis

NICOLINE ISACSON AND GREGER HELIN

Introduction

Working with children and families in empowering ways is a demanding task. We have sought to innovate in our practice in order to give parents and children more say in what happens to them when professionals become involved in their lives. The way we have done this is to attempt to embed families in their communities and let the practitioners respond more effectively to the agenda set by the families that they work with.

The topic of this chapter concerns the work we as social workers have been doing with families since the beginning of the 1980s. We have been employed in a suburb of southern Stockholm called Brånnkyrka. At that time, it had a population of about 36,000. Most of our work was concentrated on one part of Brånnkyrka, Östberga, a residential area populated predominantly by immigrant families and low-income Swedish families. The social problems were enormous and a number of children were taken into care every year.

Up until January 1997, Greater Stockholm was divided into 18 administrative districts. Since then, Stockholm has been reorganised and divided up into 24 public administrative districts. Each district is run by its own local council which makes decisions about questions covering school, day care, care of elderly people, psychiatry, culture and social welfare. We now work in the district of Älvsjö, a suburb with 20,000 inhabitants. Älvsjö used to be a part of Brånnkyrka under the old division. Östberga no longer lies in this jurisdiction and now falls outside of our remit.

Usually, when working with families and groups we try to get two outsiders to act as 'mirrors', that is, persons who are willing to reflect upon what is happening and reflect back to us what they observe in the on-going process. We, therefore, ask that the reader seeks two other volunteer readers who would be willing to share with them and us their personal reflections at the end of the chapter. Also, as English is not our first language, we hope that you will be patient with us and let us know if there is anything you do not understand. Much of our work has to do with developing our clients' personal resources, and we hope that you will all do the same for us, perhaps by writing to us with your views.

When you find your volunteers, let them introduce themselves to you and tell you where they come from, where they work, how many brothers and sisters they have, and to which social groupings they belong.

We ask you to do this because we believe that who we are as individuals affects how we operate as social workers and how well we perform our jobs. That is why it is important to us to ask you to be explicit about your values and to put effort into learning what has shaped your lives. We have to do likewise with ours.

We will now move on to recount our experience in empowering children and families through a community-based approach in a small part of Stockholm, Sweden - Älvsjö.

Background

In 1982 a new law, called the Social Services Act, came into effect in Sweden. This Act specifies that when working with people, professionals must keep the whole picture in mind. This means working on three levels: the individual, the interpersonal/group and the structural. However, the Act provided no guidelines for how the work on these three levels was to be carried out.

It soon became evident that, in practice, social workers concentrated their efforts on the individual level; the field assistants on the group level; and their superiors, supervisors, community workers and administrative staff on the structural level. Yet, no one had a grasp of the whole picture. Nor was there any communication between officials and practitioners at the different levels.

Our desire to work in a different way came about one day in January 1983, when we received a report that six youths from Östberga, all between 15 and 16 years of age, had been apprehended by the police for breaking and entering into several railway cars. They had stolen equipment worth a large amount of money and were consequently being held in custody.

We were asked to intervene and contacted the parents of these youths. Each parent blamed the other families for getting their boys into trouble. We then visited the youths in jail. Here we learnt that they had known one another since early childhood. Some had even gone to the same pre-school together.

Rather than working with this case in the traditional way by concentrating on the 'symptom bearers' and their parents, we decided to take a different approach. The methodology we adopted is described in the account which follows. We deal with the issues we covered on the three different levels first. We begin with a consideration of the individual dimension.

On the Individual Level

To commence our work with individuals, we adopted these steps:

1. We got the whole family, including siblings and other family members, to agree to meet with us once a week.
2. We arranged for the youths to each have a person they could meet on a regular basis, their own contact person to talk with and who could help to get them involved in meaningful activities. All of the contact persons came from the youths' own social networks and could be anyone from one of their former teachers to an instructor they had at summer camp.

On the Interpersonal Level

These interventions were followed by the third step which was aimed at enhancing interpersonal relationships:

3. We offered all six sets of parents the opportunity to meet together once every 14 days to discuss their parental roles.

At first, the parents were reluctant to meet with us. They had many preconceived ideas about other families in the group, even though their own children had often been visitors in the homes of the other families. The majority of the families had had or still had dealings with the social services and had acquired a very negative opinion about public authorities in general.

After a couple of sessions for each youth, we succeeded in getting both parents to attend the meetings, whether they lived together or not. If a youth's biological father was unavailable, the stepfather came in his stead. We talked about many things, such as the parents' experiences of their own childhood and adolescence, what they saw as their parental role, and what kind of reception they had received from various public authorities across the years.

As we worked with the parents in a group, it soon came to light that several of them had felt that their authority had been subverted by public officials as far back as when their children were in day care. They had been deprived of their parental authority and their sons had witnessed their humiliation over the years. Consequently, the boys had lost all respect for their parents. As we worked together, the idea grew in the group to give them back their parental authority. The parents formulated a set of rules and norms which were to apply to all the youths in the group; for example, keeping to meal-times, honouring curfews, paying for their keep at home if they had a job, and so forth.

After the third meeting, the youths began to congregate outside the door of the meeting-room, asking to come in! They were not used to their parents going to meetings from which they were excluded and they demanded to be allowed to attend. Developments in the meetings led to a situation where the parents began to assert their parental role. This provided the basis for step number four:

4. As an additional support for the parents, we agreed to accompany them to meetings with various public officials.

We met with staff from the youth recreation centre to hear their opinion of the boys. We invited school staff and the police to come to the parents' meetings and give their views. Our activities in this dimension led to the enlargement of the parents' support networks and constituted the next step in our proceedings. Thus:

5. Each family gathered its network together to talk about the problems and see what kind of support the persons closest to them could offer.

During one month we could come into contact with up to 250 persons who were involved, one way or another, with our families. Most of these people had a positive attitude to being contacted by us because they were already involved and felt concern. Having achieved this degree of integration of parents into their local support systems, we moved onto the third level of intervention. Influencing developments at the structural level, constituted the basis of our endeavours for the sixth step. However, addressing this level posed its own problems, including those of carrying our own management with us:

Structural Level

6. In our written reports to the local council, we described how the families had been adversely affected by the shortcomings of the society.

We made a serious effort to describe the kinds of difficulties that arise in raising children if the public authorities concerned are non-cooperative and non-supportive. But our own administrative personnel cut those passages out of our reports, stating that they could hardly have relevance for the council members!

To overcome minor setbacks such as these, we decided to be innovative and draw on other mediums of communication than the written word. The audio-visual domain seemed to us to fit our requirements. The making of videos to highlight the plight of our clients became the seventh step in our proceedings:

7. We made video films of our families in which they could tell their own stories.

The impact of this novel approach was gratifying. The local councillors had never set foot in the area they administered. Indeed, they lived in another part of the district and knew little about it. We felt that it was important that they get an idea of what the people living in the area thought and felt. People whose life situation is already vulnerable, whose self-confidence has already taken a severe beating, may find it hard to speak in front of public officials and civil servants. We had the possibility of documenting the course of daily life of these families and picking up on the issues they wanted to ventilate to those in power through videos.

We got the councillors interested in what was happening in this district and succeeded in maintaining their attention for several years afterwards. Moreover, this approach had positive results for our families. For as a result of our efforts, the youth recreational sector received extra funding during this time.

However, the work we were doing with our families was becoming cumbersome. Their interaction with a range of different professionals needed better co-ordination and streamlining. From trying to solve this problem, we came up with the idea of dividing our families into age-based groups. This act became the basis for our next step:

8. Division into groups by age.

If the parents had problems of their own in the form of economic problems, unemployment, substance abuse, and at the same time had children in day care or school, they could have up to 17 different civil servants and public officials involved in how they conducted their lives. These persons in authority seldom had any contact with one another and often had different ideas about what kind of help the family needed. On those occasions when the public authorities had contact with one another, a lot of time was often lost in fruitless conflicts. In the meantime, the families were fully occupied with having to keep in touch with them all.

We arranged a two-day seminar and invited a wide range of public authorities and non-profit organisations to come and give us their views on Östberga. They were divided into groups based on the ages of the individuals who came under their jurisdiction - children and adults. This gave us the following age groups: 0-6 years, 7-12 years, 13-20 years and 20-100 years.

The groups formed at the seminar continued to meet once a month to discuss developments in their residential area and to find quicker ways to help children and families who were having difficulties. An immediate advantage was that those who worked with the residents in the area got to know one another and new co-workers became familiar very quickly with the social and economic structure of the area.

The frequency of public placements for children in care dropped radically as a result, largely because a large group of persons were brought into the work of supporting each other at an early stage.

The improved communication between practitioners however, revealed another weakness in our system. This was the problem of authority to make decisions that more appropriately belonged to a higher level, but needing to influence these in ways which produced desired outcomes for the families with whom we were working. Responding to this difficulty prompted us to form groups for the managers and supervisors responsible for those who had front line contact with our families. This resulted in step nine of our programme:

9. Work groups for managers and supervisors.

It soon became evident that those of us in the field had no authority to decide on the changes that had to be made in Östberga to create a better life for the inhabitants. We suggested, therefore, that those who held supervisory positions within the public authorities in question meet regularly with their managers in order to keep them informed about events on the front line and to make the decisions that were needed on the structural level.

The field assistants kept their own supervisors informed. But we were also able to submit joint proposals regarding issues pertinent to Östberga. That we were successful can be largely attributed to the faith the local councillors had in us as a result of the video films we had shown them about Östberga.

Our successes at this point led us to consider an area which had been largely peripheral to our day-to-day concerns up to this point. That is, developing a useful and helpful connection between what we were doing on the ground and the research and preparation of the practitioners of the future which was being conducted in our neighbouring institutions of higher learning. Our enthusiasm in doing something about this led to step number ten.

10. Establishing links between the education of social workers and the field in theory, practice and research.

Through the years we had given some thought to the extent to which education and training in our profession corresponded to actual conditions in the field. Therefore, in 1984, we offered to serve as a district mentor for a class of students attending the basic course in social work at Stockholm University. This was expanded to comprise five terms during which the students, in addition to their work at the University, attended lectures held a couple of times a week in the district. These lectures were prepared by field assistants together with the students themselves and teachers from the University. The students formed groups of six persons which met regularly together with two social workers to discuss topics they themselves proposed. These included everything from the linkage between theory and practice, topical social issues, and the social worker role to the students' personal worries about successfully completing their education. The first practice term which was a 20-credit training course comprising the third term of their education, was decentralised to the local district. So far, we have followed three successive basic qualifying social work education classes for a period of five years.

We have named our project, *Close Contact*, which means working with what is impossible to achieve the possible. After having worked for a couple of years as supervisors for the social workers in Östberga, we were ready to try something new. We had in the meantime completed our training as network therapists and had the competence to arrange and carry out large-scale crisis meetings. We submitted a proposal to work with families coming from two other residential areas that had become a part of our district under the reorganisation of 1997. The target group was families with children aged between 0 and 20 years.

The idea, basically, was to offer our services in doing intensive work with families whose children were a cause for serious concern. The parents had the option of refusing to work with us, or of accepting. If they accepted, a contract was drawn up for a two-month period, after which time the contract was reviewed together with the family's caseworker. The family could break off contact with us whenever they wished, in which case the caseworker resumed control and took responsibility for working out other alternatives.

Working with us became a viable option for the placement of many of the families during the 4 years and 3 months that Project *Close Contact* was in effect. The Project's approach was to work intensively, in close contact with the families and their social networks, in the families' own homes. In all, we came into contact with about 120 children during this time. Seven of the children had to be taken into care. Two of these came from the same family. The social worker had wanted to take these two children into care earlier, but was afraid to do anything overtly because the mother had threatened the staff with a gun. The parents were heavily into substance abuse and after a couple of network meetings, the network gave up. Today, these parents are 'clean'. They are conscientious towards their children and it is their opinion that it was fortunate that their children were taken into care.

Four of the other seven children taken into care lived with a mother who suffered from mental ill health. For years, she had been threatening to kill herself and her children. As she was unable to function as a mother for the children, they were placed in a foster home. However, this intervention produced a mixed outcome.

The last child in the group, a girl of thirteen, was taken into care because she did not keep her end of the bargain and ran away from home instead. Her social worker and her parents saw no other solution than to place the girls in an institution where her case could be reviewed regularly.

The United Nations Convention on the Rights of the Child

We also felt that we needed to intervene at the national level by drawing upon international agreements relating to the rights of children. The opportunity to do this arose in relation to commitments Sweden entered into with the United Nations. The work in this arena involved us in the activities we describe below. Our first step was the following:

1. In 1991, the social services sector of Stockholm was engaged in drawing up an action plan for working in accordance with the United Nations (UN) conventions on children's rights. In this connection, we offered to conduct a study which used a questionnaire to ascertain what the various public authorities engaged in working with children in their

districts saw as possibilities for collaboration among themselves and with other organisations.

The outcome of this piece of research was discouraging. The only group who claimed that they had a good working relationship with the other organisations was the social services sector, but none of the others thought that they had any working relationship to speak of with the social welfare officers. From this result, we decided to do something to address the situation and undertook the actions identified in steps two and three below.

2. The next step was to bring everyone together in a two-day conference to give participants the opportunity to:

   • meet face to face with others who were engaged in working with the same target group - children and adolescence;
   • get to know each other and develop new strategies;
   • listen to alternative lectures about the needs of children and adolescents.

About 250 persons attended the conference on both days. In each of the three local districts, the participants formed age-based groups that accorded with the Östbrega model detailed above because it had been proving itself successful since 1988. This initiative was subsequently followed up with a further interagency jamboree as we embarked on step three in this area:

3. In 1995, we all met again in a combined one-day workshop and seminar in which the public service organisations presented their activities for one another and shared experiences.

   The discussions we had then revealed another gap in the provisions for administrative and professional training which we sought to address as specified in step four:

4. Social network training.

The various groups of personnel attending the workshop and seminar soon realised that there was a need for a joint education and training programme.

We had trained personnel in various sectors of Östberga in networking earlier and therefore, we felt we could offer the three social districts an 8-day training programme in this method of work. The participants invited to take part in the programme came from all of the public authorities, organisations, clubs and associations involved in the three districts.

Three groups were formed as a result of these deliberations. Two of these had 30 participants each and the third 60 participants. At first, the participants were suspicious of one another and the training programme, but as the programme progressed, those from the various public authorities began to collaborate in setting up joint projects. A lot of the time was devoted to learning about one another's professional areas of operation, who we were as individuals and the values that directed our lives.

For each group, the 8-day programme concluded with a study trip to a European country - Parma, Italy; Barcelona, Spain; and London, England. The study trip gave the participants a further opportunity to make a systematic study of children and their families in places which used different approaches in addressing similar problems.

Developments in the Local Council District of Älvsjö

As mentioned above, the public administration of Stockholm was reorganised in January 1997, and now consists of 24 rather than 18 administrative districts. Today, the district of Älvsjö extends over about a third of its former area and Östberga belongs to another district entirely.

Since January 1997, Greger Helin has become a member of the steering group for the new administrative district of Älvsjö and is responsible for co-ordinating questions pertaining to children and adolescents. He has no budget of his own and no staff. He is aided by Nicoline Isacson who has been employed until the end of 1997, as Project Head for the projects that have been developed through his work. The work that they have carried out comes under the auspices of what has been termed the BUA Project. In English, this translates into the Assess, Execute and Identify Alternatives Project. Its coming into existence constituted our first step:

1. The Assess, Execute and Identify Alternatives (BUA) Project is a joint programme for the education and training of persons appointed as a special resource personnel to work with children with special needs.

Today, there are 5 groups in operation with 10 participants each who meet regularly to discuss better and quicker ways to help distressed families. The groups are multi-professionally based and include people from mother health care centres (MVC), child health care centres (BVC), the child welfare authorities, the school programme for six-year olds, special resource persons from all three levels of the obligatory schooling including psychologists, counsellors, school nurses and school leaders, field assistants, supervisors from youth recreational centres and the playground programmes, and lastly, social workers. The object is to find common ground for working with and relating to children's needs. We also provide training in counselling interview techniques. In all we do, we have a genuine curiosity about the people with whom we interact.

As a child goes through life he or she encounters many persons in official positions who can see that things are not as they should be in the child's life. One sees, but at the same time may feel, that there is perhaps not quite enough evidence to warrant an intervention. And so, the child wanders from one public service institution to another and no one readily reacts or intervenes, although many have devoted considerable time and energy to worrying about the child. In the meantime, relatives, friends, and neighbours all wonder what is going on and if there is any way that they can help. And while the family, in the best of cases, may be aware of the others' concern, often they have never even been asked if they want help. The table we have constructed below depicts the range of agencies which intervene in children's lives at different ages. Their range also gives an idea about how important it is to have good communications amongst them all if the interests of children are to be served well.

Table 1   Agencies Encountered by Children at Different Ages

MVC	BVC	Child care	PBU	School Counsellor	Psychologist	school nurse	spec. resource person	field ass't	youth centre	police	social services
0	2 yrs		6 yrs	10 years		12 years		14 yrs			16 yrs

Our successes up to this point, however, led us to feel that we need to have a physical resource for our activities which could provide a base for our families to congregate and symbolise their achievements. This led us to develop a network house which became the second step in our strategy of helping our families.

2. Network house in Älvsjö.

Starting in September 1997, Älvsjö will have its own network house to support them in the task of taking control of their lives. Children, youths and families can go there for counselling. They can get help to mobilise the important persons in their social network and get them to meet to discuss their situation. Family treatment and family counselling sessions can also be arranged. There is an open pre-school where parents can go with their children up to 2 years of age before they enter the ordinary pre-school programme. This gives them the opportunity to get an early start in the educational stakes. There is also a field assistant assigned to that district. Help is provided in the running of the various child care activities and BUA groups can get advice and support from the Network House which has the responsibility of keeping abreast of what is taking place in the area.

Whilst developing this aspect of our work, we have continued with our interest in social work qualifying training. The outcome of our efforts in this area are also about to bear fruit in a significant way as we describe below.

3. Educational centre.

Through the years we have seen how difficult it is to find ways to collaborate across areas of competence. Although we have been engaged in providing training and education programmes for public authorities, we are still trying to find new ways to facilitate co-operation. We believe that this question is important enough to warrant being a part of the qualifying training programme for social workers. During 1997, we have had negotiations with colleges that train subject teachers, youth recreational counsellors, pre-school teachers and graduate social workers. Beginning with the fall of 1998, we plan to participate in these education programmes from the very first day, and in the same way as we did in the programmes offered by the School of Social Work at the University of Stockholm. The big difference now is that all practice is to take place in the social district and that from the very beginning the students will learn forms of co-operation and get a better idea of the other professionals' competences so that they will understand how best to use the other professions. Networking and interagency co-operation are to be principles that pervade all aspects of socially oriented work in those districts and professional schools with which we have a working relationship.

Conclusion

In conclusion, we want to say that we enjoy our work. We find it stimulating. Sometimes, forces have worked against us, but what has helped to keep us going through the years is that we (Nicoline Isacson and Greger Helin) work well together and share a common goal. Furthermore, there are distinct advantages to men and women working together as a team. It has not always been easy, and we have provoked quite a few people in our time. But we have also been able to get to where we are today because of our collaboration together.

And now, for our mirrors! What is your feedback?

9 Empowering Children: The End-Point for Community Approaches to Child Welfare

LENA DOMINELLI

Introduction

Community approaches to child welfare offer considerable opportunities for a range of innovations and developments which have the potential to shift the balance of power in client-practitioner relationships towards the less powerful part of the partnership - the service users. Altering power relations in this way is crucial to the empowerment of children and their parents. However, professionals should not delude themselves by thinking that this will either be easy or that new forms of inequality will not seep into their interactions with those with whom they work, despite their intentions to the contrary.

This chapter concludes *Community Approaches to Child Welfare* by focusing on power relations in professional interactions between clients and workers, considering the empowerment of children, and identifying the agenda for internationalising social work practice with children and families.

Power Relations in Professional Partnerships

Replacing power relations at the client-worker interface is a complex business because power emanates from a number of different sources, each of which contributes to the creation of particular arrangements in the interchanges people have with one another. Because there is a dynamic interaction between them, each of these will alter if any one part of the power relation is changed. Moreover, since power relations are created through interpersonal interactions, all those involved in the relationship contribute to its formation and reformation as part of an on-going process of social intercourse.

Even though children and parents may have less power than the professionals working with them because they do not have access to the variety of resources, particularly in the form of funding and enabling legislation, that the practitioners do, they still have other sources of power which they can and do draw upon to ensure that their status is not simply a disempowered one. These include their knowledge of themselves, their ability to form networks and relationships with others in the community and the 'savoir faire' they have of the systems within which they operate (see Dominelli, 1986; Dominelli and Gollins, 1997).

In chapter eight, Nicoline Isacson and Greger Helin indicate the complexity of levels to be tackled when building new professional relationships which attempt to shift the balance of power in the direction of those disadvantaged by the social order. In it, they also demonstrate the painstaking negotiations that have to take place for their ideas to yield promise. They also reveal how the problem of institutional abuse - in this case of the disempowerment of parents in the eyes of their children, has to be specifically addressed. They do so in a way that re-asserts parental authority within the family setting whilst encouraging the formation of an enabling community partnership that involves children, parents, professionals, the community at large and local politicians. From their efforts, they conclude that a substantial degree of social change can be enacted through the development of a helpful partnership between practitioners and the families within which they work, especially if these are able to attract community representatives to their activities. Bringing the policy makers on side has the potential to endow their work with greater legitimacy and extra funding. Moreover, their enterprise indicates that a considerable amount of social change can be brought about by taking a community orientation to problem-solving.

Similarly, Marilyn Taylor in chapter seven, demonstrates how important it is to treat young people like Tracey as sentient beings with decision-making capacities and skills which should be promoted, not hindered, by professional intervention. Supporting young people's initiative facilitates their acquisition of greater skills, a growth in confidence and the development of their personalities. Achieving this form of support also calls for a reconceptualisation of the idea of who is 'fit to assist' another person. In the particular situation cited, the failure of the birth family and the professionals to rally to Penny's aid brought in peer networks to the cause *after* professional resistance had been overcome. By taking a more active role in fostering these links, practitioners can contribute to young people feeling more empowered through their own initiatives.

Thus, as Tracey's story indicates, bureaucratic and legislative forms of power are critical in the client-worker relationship. However, they do not have to be taken as having the ultimate say in how practitioners work with those in their charge. Empowerment requires that personal power be considered as one of several important sources of self-realisation.

However, the lessons that can be derived from chapter three by Marilyn Callahan and chapter four by Bill Lee make it clear that personal power cannot be taken as the be all and end all of interactions. Managerial intervention, globalisation and resourcing levels all contribute to the extent to which individuals can of and by themselves alter their circumstances. Weighting the scales too heavily in the personal direction runs the danger of pathologising the service users and denying them the contributions that they make as individuals drawing on their own particular strengths.

However, these two chapters demonstrate the importance of validating the work that service users undertake in overcoming the hurdles and bureaucratic inertia which the organisation of professional practice has drawn in its wake. Marilyn Callahan's research in particular, demonstrates the *personal price* that women pay in devoting their energies to tackling the obstacles planted in their path by poverty and the reactions of agency personnel purportedly there to assist them. But lest we forget, the workers too are victims of managerialist and social forces beyond their immediate control.

A lesson to be taken from this study which is backed by the findings in Joan Gilroy's as well, is that both workers and clients need to empower themselves and assert their views and control over a system that has strayed from delivering the care that it promises. Moreover, as the Mi'kmaq experience indicates, rising to such a challenge requires a community approach which involves everyone in the task of creating and owning the agencies set up to deliver care. Getting to this stage also necessitates attitudinal changes on the individual, group and political levels. Discussing issues of reciprocity, interdependence and accountability are initial steps in this process.

The validity of an approach which releases the capacities of parents is also affirmed by Shirley Jackson and Paul Nixon in chapter six where they argue for the Family Group Conference as the way forward in redressing power imbalances between professionals and the parents they purport to serve. Its significance is also evident in the pleas that Marilyn Callahan makes in asking that citizenship be redefined to acknowledge the strengths that welfare clients have and which they utilise to negotiate the hurdles they encounter in their daily lives. A citizenship of the whole is no greater than its weakest link. The exclusion of large numbers of women and children through poverty cheapens the expression of citizenship for those living in affluence.

Yet, despite their ideals, Mehmoona Moosa-Mitha's chapter indicates how far short of their aspirations, social workers can reach when seeking to develop new forms of partnerships with children and their families. Children in care still receive a raw deal despite the fine words conveyed in policy documents. The denial of their human rights in this way is an indictment of the caring system provided by the communities in which these children live.

The main group that has been poorly represented in the discussions about empowerment within the leaves of this book is that of the children and young people themselves. Although Nicoline Isacson and Greger Helin mention the Convention on the Rights of the Child, little is said about children's rights from children's own perspectives in their contribution. Rather, theirs, alongside the writings of several other authors in this collection have focused on children's positions within their families and the rights of parents rather than the state to decide what should happen to them. In these, they have implied that parental direction is likely to be more conducive to children's well-being than either professional or state intervention carried out through its employees - a point that cannot be taken for granted.

However, these do not assume that the parents are necessarily the birth parents. Social parenting can and does have its place. But, the state's role is seen as a limited one which is enacted primarily in situations in which paternalistic parents have failed to meet their obligations. Whilst distancing the state is an important dimension of the problem of redressing the imbalance of power between professionals and their clients. I would argue that it is insufficient for those seeking to ensure that the balance of power between children and their parents or carers is more favourably adjusted for children. Thus, empowering children in their own terms remains a project for the future.

Empowering Children

Community approaches to child welfare can be useful in pursuing the objective of empowering children because these can make caring for children a responsibility that can be discharged by a large group of people which are not necessarily related to children through kinship ties, but who, nonetheless, accept that they have a duty of care towards them. These people are those living in the same community as them and who share with them a number of attributes and social links rooted in interdependence, reciprocity and citizenship. For adults to share a reciprocated interdependent citizenship with children requires the empowerment of children, that is, their being treated as citizens from birth.

Children's upbringing, therefore, becomes one of their realising their rights as citizens from day one with the assistance of adults until they are able to do things for themselves. The process whereby this happens will vary for each individual child for it has to cater for his or her uniqueness as well as group identity. However, it is conducted as a publicly accountable process in which a child never loses his or her citizenship rights and entitlements. Thus, the child may exist in a family, but that family is not a unitary one in which individual needs are subsumed for the whole. A process of reciprocated accommodation between one individual and the others who make up the whole unit is an essential element within this set-up.

Thus, community perspectives contain the possibility of making children less directly dependent on their parents and hold forth the promise that children will not be treated as *belonging* to their parents in a proprietorial sense. Social workers have a role to play in ensuring that the rights of children are maintained and that their voice is heard.

The fact that children do have difficulties in being listened to by adults because they may be of a young age or vulnerable makes it even more imperative that parents and non-parents alike respect their rights and go out of their way to provide an environment that promotes children's creativity, decision-making capacities and growth to their full potential. A community that cares for its children will be a community whose children will ultimately care for it. This becomes another way in which the social reciprocity that Marilyn Callahan described in chapter three can be enhanced. Additionally, the disproportionate burden of care that social workers carry with regards to children that Joan Gilroy spoke so eloquently about in chapter two will also be lessened if all adults in the communities that children live within care for them in a reciprocal and reciprocated manner whether or not they are their biological parents. This expression of care does not have to be in the form of direct face-to-face contact. It can be discharged formally through transfer payments and taxation to provide the wherewithal needed to keep children out of poverty and free from violence. It can also be supplemented informally through voluntary activities at the organisational level.

Involving the community as a whole and working in partnership with its members can also be empowering for the practitioners. For instead of one lone professional working in a poorly resourced office with an under-resourced and over-stressed mother, each and every member of the community would be contributing towards making the world a better a place for children. If this were to happen, children would be truly cherished and could be helped to grow in ways that would enable them to reach their ultimate limits. The empowerment of children, can in this way, contribute to the empowerment of parents.

International Initiatives in Child Welfare

Internationalising child welfare can occur on two levels. One of these is in the agreement about and enforcement of children's right to healthy growth as citizens. The other is in dealing with the social problems that afflict children and are global in nature. In this context, international law can assist in the promotion of children's rights as to the type of care and material support that facilitates their development into adulthood. The provisions currently enshrined in the Convention on the Rights of the Child provide a step towards this goal. However, having common principles of this general nature is not enough. Ways have to be found to enforce their realisation. Because achieving this state of affairs may require a redistribution of resources from rich to poor, from North to South, the turning of parenting from a private matter into a public one, a considerable number of hurdles will have to be overcome.

However, each adult could begin this process by ensuring that poverty in childhood is eradicated in the specific countries that each personally inhabits and by initiating a discussion on social parenting. In short, a community approach to child welfare requires that each adult puts some effort into sustaining the growth and development of all children in their locality. These efforts can also be internationalised through the formation of international organisations that have specific tasks vis-a-vis children. Eradicating child poverty would be a good one to tackle first because even though doing so has to incorporate the direct voice of the child more explicitly and forcefully than hitherto, much of the necessary framework is already in place. Moreover, these initiatives need to include children in industrialised countries as well as those in industrialising ones for interdependence and reciprocity stretch across the globe.

In addition, adults need to ensure that they cater for the rich diversity of human forms of social organisation which can be found throughout the world. The cloning of dominant forms is inappropriate in either a national or international context. Thus, their endeavours have to address both diversities and commonalities. Adults - whether parents, practitioners or non-parenting members of the lay public, will have to focus on how to discover: what can be the common principles of intervention to which all peoples on this planet can subscribe; which pieces of legislation can be enacted that have global support and enforceability; what practice methods can be used to ensure that universally agreed standards of care are guaranteed for each and every child regardless of the living arrangements in which he or she is embedded; and what is the appropriate balance amongst the competing interests of children, parents, non-parenting adults and the state, in which the child resides.

The problems to be overcome will be both ideological and practical. Shifting adult public opinion towards the view that whether they are parents or not, they have a responsibility towards children whom they may have never met and in whose life they have no direct involvement will be a major obstacle to movement forward. Attaining it will require extensive debates, public education, political conviction and a commitment of resources towards its realisation. Convincing children that their dependence on adults does not have to be a major barrier to their taking control over many aspects of their lives from a very young age will not happen automatically. Likewise, ensuring that children and adults become aware of the interdependent nature of intergenerational relationships and how these will change across the life cycle will be no easy task in those countries accustomed to endorsing sharp distinctions between childhood and adulthood.

There have been attempts to deal with some of these issues already. Indeed, organisations such as the United Nations have a number of agencies looking into some of the issues affecting children. The United Nations Children's Fund (UNICEF) has crucial responsibilities in promoting the interests of children. The United Nations Educational, Scientific and Cultural Organisation (UNESCO) also takes a key role in this regard, although its remit is fairly broad. Others, such as United Nations Commission on Human Rights (UNHCR) consider children in more specific crisis situations such as refugee children who have escaped from war-torn zones. Nonetheless, the basic framework which these have established is patchy and its powers weak. Thus, in their implementation agreed legislation, policies and conventions have been violated even by signatory countries which have pledged to do the contrary.

As a result of these failures in the past, the UN has launched a review of its structures and powers and sought to encourage the realisation of its various initiatives. Individual countries have initiated their own programmes vis-a-vis children. In Canada, for example, Campaign 2000 seeks to eliminate child poverty by the turn of the century when signatories to the Convention on the Rights of the Child will meet to monitor progress on the global implementation of the commitments regarding children outlined in 1989. As Isacson and Helin indicate in their chapter, practitioners in Sweden have begun their own evaluations of its progress. Britain has yet to commence programmes which hold a similar status although the Blairite Labour government has pledged to deal with social exclusion as part of its new contract with the British people.

Meanwhile, social workers can advocate extensively in this area. They are the professionals with a specific mandate to address the needs of children and their families in each of the countries considered in this book. And, they are all too aware from their daily practice of the obstacles that parents and other adults who care for children have to overcome in order to provide a decent life for them. They can, therefore, collect the research data necessary for mounting a powerful case in support of every child's right to have the wherewithal necessary for their development to their full potential guaranteed by the state in which they live. Adults will be able to contribute to this project through the taxation system and by playing a more active role in ensuring that their community environment is a child-centred one. The experiences of First Nations peoples described in Joan Gilroy's chapter, the work undertaken by the Children's Aid Society in Toronto which is the focus of Bill Lee's contribution and the work of Nicoline Isacson and Greger Helin in Stockholm reveal that such an approach is possible in small community settings. The bigger challenge will be the extent to which such endeavours can be generalised and globalised.

Conclusion

Children's rights rooted in a universalism based on the acknowledgement of intergenerational interdependence and solidarities is a main way forward for a future in which globalisation has shrunk the 'territories' which divide one country from another and which has made permeable the boundaries of the nation-state.

The specific demands of a child-centred interdependent model of solidarity would require that each child receives:

a. A guaranteed income in his or her own right even if an adult administers it on behalf of a child during infancy. Child benefit and family allowances as currently constituted in those Western countries which have them are still considered the parent's income because the family is considered as a unitary whole. The family needs to be reconceptualised as both unitary and fragmented by the diverse interests and social divisions operating within it.

b. Appropriate housing, health care and education.

c. A physical environment which can sustain his or her healthy development to adulthood.

d. Portable citizenship rights regardless of place of abode.

e. Intergenerational solidarity or reciprocated commitment to caring for all members of the community throughout the life cycle.

Thus, in return for being cared for, a child would reciprocate in adulthood by supporting those who are then dependent on their community for assistance whether they be children or adults. During childhood, learning about reciprocity in their interaction with others would enable young people to make a smooth transition to caring for others in their own adulthood.

The empowerment of children becomes an integral part of this broader agenda of handling the transition from childhood to adulthood as a socially negotiated process which includes children as equal partners. Treating them as equal partners does not mean that they are like (little) adults in any respect. But it does mean that their right to make decisions for themselves is something that is to be taken as given, but which is helped to develop to maturity in every daily interaction the child has. The realisation of this goal carries considerable implications for adults whether or not they are parents, and for welfare professionals. It is a challenge to the unfettered paternalism of both parents and the state, although it seeks to steer a course away from the view that children are not also accountable to and responsible for others.

As a result, childhood is accorded a special status without falling into the trap of conceptualising children as little adults. Instead, it is accepted that children are people in the process of becoming adults from the day that they are born. But this period is also seen as a historical event which is socially constructed through the interaction between children and adults and mediated by the state in the country in which they live although this can and in certain circumstances should be internationalised. The model also endorses a welfare focused approach. The welfare of the child and his or her right to develop to adult maturity is the cornerstone upon which children's empowerment is based. All adults, regardless of whether they are parents or not, share in the social obligation of launching the child into the future as a well-adjusted citizen capable of making his or her own decisions about his or her life. Thus, in empowering children, adults also contribute to their empowerment as better parents.

This conceptualisation of childhood also challenges the current notion of citizenship which is a status that is acquired as one grows up and is limited to being exercised within the boundaries of the nation-state. Instead, citizenship is conceived as something a child is born with and which is transported with him or her wherever he or she may subsequently live. But whilst society has obligations towards its children, children have a reciprocal duty towards the society in which they live, regardless of the length of time they reside within it. That is, that they also contribute to its endeavours to an increasing degree as they reach adulthood.

Community approaches to child welfare that aim to treat children as equal citizens require adults to facilitate children's decision-making capacities at all points in their growth curve. Facilitating the healthy development of children as they make the transition from childhood into adulthood necessitates a partnership that involves children, parents, other adults who are not parents and the state participating in it. The key aim of this partnership is that of enabling children to move from one status to another in a supportive and supported manner. Whilst parents, particularly birth parents and their extended families are likely to play a major role in this process, they will not be allowed to undertake their tasks without being held publicly accountable for their actions, nor will they be unsupported in their efforts by being expected to do it all.

In short, the division between public matters and private ones will be recognised as an interdependent and permeable one. Changes in one realm will influence developments in the other. Thus, for example, supporting parents in the home may carry implications for their being supported in the workplace. Sweden's child care policy has begun to make some of these connections by enabling either mothers or fathers to take parental leave when children are born or sick. However, it still treats the family in a unitary manner and requires parents to split the time between them, thereby allowing gender inequalities to persist because women's earning capacity in the labour force, though better than in many other countries, is still not equivalent to men's. In addition, adults will be restrained from exercising their power in an arbitrary manner by the emphasis on children being involved in decision-making throughout their lives. The state's use of arbitrary power will be monitored by both adults and children working in the partnership.

The way before us is clear. Will adults have the courage to embark upon it?

References

Dominelli, L. (1986), 'The Power of the Powerless: Prostitution and the Reinforcement of Submissive Femininity', *Sociological Review*, vol. 34, no. 1, pp. 65-92.

Dominelli, L. and Gollins, T. (1997), 'Men, Power and Caring Relationships', *Sociological Review*, vol. 45, no. 3, August, pp. 396-415.

United Nations Development Programme (UNDP) (1998), *Human Development Report, 1998*, United Nations, New York.

Bibliography

Ackhurst, B. A. (1975), 'The Prevalence of Behaviour Problems among Children in Care', *Educational Research*, vol. 17, pp. 137-142.

Adamson, N., Briskin, L. and McPhail, M. (1989), *Feminist Organising for Change*, Oxford University Press, Toronto.

Aldgate, J., Tunstill, J., Ozolins, R. and McBeath, G. (1994), *Family Support and the Children Act: The First Eighteen Months - A Report to the Department of Health*, University of Leicester, School of Social Work, Leicester.

Alinsky, S. (1971), *Rules for Radicals*, Vintage Press, New York.

Aries, P. (1962), *Centuries of Childhood*, Penguin, Harmondsworth.

Atkin, W. R. (1989), 'New Zealand: Children versus Families - Is there any Conflict?' *Journal of Family Law*, vol. 27, pp. 231-40.

Audit Commission (1994), *Seen but not Heard*, HMSO, London.

Bagley, C. and Thurston, E. (1996), *Understanding and Preventing Child Sexual Abuse: Critical summaries of 500 Key Studies*, Arena, Aldershot.

Barber, C. (1994), *Playing by the Rules: An Evaluation of Child Protection Services in Hampshire*, Hampshire County Council, Winchester.

Barbour, A. (1991), 'Family Group Conferences: Context and Consequences', *Social Work Review*, vol. 3, no. 4, pp. 5-6.

Barn, R. (1990), 'Black Children in Local Authority Care: Admission Patterns', *New Community*, vol. 16, no. 2, pp. 14-28.

Barn, R . (1993a), 'Black and White Care Careers: A Different Reality' in P. Marsh and J. Triseliotis (eds), *Prevention and Reunification in Child Care*, Batsford, London.

Barn, R. (1993b), *Black Children in Care*, Batsford, London.

Barr, D. (1971), 'Doing Prevention', *Ontario Association of Children's Aid Society Journal*, February, pp. 8-13.

Barr, D. (1979), 'The Regent Park Community Service Unit: Partnership can Work', in B. Wharf (ed), *Community Work in Canada*, McClelland and Stewart, Toronto, pp. 27-50.

Barr, D. and McLaughlin, A. (1975), 'A Community Worker Prevention Programme', *Ontario Association of Children's Aid Society Journal*, April.

Beamish, C. and Lee, B. (1973), 'Catholic Children's Aid Society (CCAS) and

Native People', *Ontario Association of Children's Aid Society Journal*, January, pp. 9-11.

Bell, S. (1987), *When Salem Came to the Boro'*, Penguin, Harmondsworth.

Benn, C. (1981), *Attacking Poverty through Participation*, PIT Publishing, Melbourne.

Berridge, D. (1997), *Foster Care: A Research Review*, HMSO, London.

Berridge, D. and Cleaver, H. (1987), *Foster Home Breakdown*, Blackwell, Oxford.

Biddle, W. and Biddle, L. (1965), *The Community Development Process*, Rinehart and Winston, New York.

Bishop, A. (1994), *Becoming an Ally*, Fernwood Publishing, Halifax.

Bonnerjea, L. (1990), *Leaving Care in London*, London Children's Regional Planning Committee, London.

Brager, G., Specht, H. and Torczyner, J.L. (1987), *Community Organising*, Columbia University Press, New York.

Brodie, J. (1996), 'Restructuring and the New Citizenship', in I. Bakker (ed), *Rethinking Restructuring: Gender and Change in Canada*, University of Toronto Press, Toronto.

Bullock, R., Little, M. and Millham, S. (1993), *Going Home: The Return of Children Separated from their Families*, Dartmouth, Aldershot:

Callahan, M. and Lumb, C. (1995), 'My Cheque and my Children: The Long Road to Empowerment in Child Welfare', in *Child Welfare*, LXXIV, no. 3, May/June, pp. 795-819.

Campbell, B. (1988), *Official Secrets*, London. Revised in 1997.

Cain, R. (1993), 'Community Based AIDS Services: Formalization and Depoliticization', *International Journal of Health Services*, no. 23, Fall, pp. 665-684.

Canadian Association of Social Workers (1994), *Social Work Code of Ethics: Amendments*, Canadian Association of Social Workers and Nova Scotia Association of Social Workers.

Cavanagh, K. and Cree, V. (1995), *Working with Men from a Feminist Perspective*, Routledge, London.

Community Worker Group (1998), *Discussion Document*, Community Worker Group, Toronto, January 7.

Connolly, M. (1994), 'An Act of Empowerment: the Children, Young Persons and their Families Act 1989', *British Journal of Social Work*, vol. 24, pp. 87-100.

Cowburn, M. and Dominelli, L. (1998), 'Beyond Litigation: False Memory Syndrome', *British Journal of Social Work*, vol., no., pp. 526-540.

Cross Branch Community Worker's Group (1980), *Framework for the Eighties. Internal Report*, Children's Aid Society of Metropolitan Toronto, Toronto.

Cross Branch Community Worker's Group (1990), *Community Work Programme Report*, Children's Aid Society of Metropolitan Toronto, Toronto.

Cross Branch Community Worker's Group (1992), *Community Work Programme Report*, Children's Aid Society of Metropolitan Toronto, Toronto.

Crow, G. and Marsh, P. (1997), *Family Group Conferences, Partnership and Child Welfare: A Research Report on Four Pilot Projects in England and Wales*, University of Sheffield Partnership Research Programme, Sheffield.

Crow, G. and Marsh, P. (1998), *Family Group Conferences in Child Welfare*, Blackwell, Oxford.

Davis, G., Messner, H., Umbreit, M.S. and Coates, R. (1992) *Making Amends: Mediation and Reparation in Criminal Justice*, Routledge , London.

Department of Community Services (1990), *Children and Family Services Act, Statutes of Nova Scotia, 1990*, Queen's Printer, Halifax.

Department of Community Services (1995), *Children and Family Services Regulations, 1995*, Queen's Printer, Halifax.

Department of Health (DoH) (1988), *Children in Care: Memorandum Laid Before the Social Services Select Committee*, HMSO, London.

Department of Health (DoH) (1989), *The Care of Children: Principles and Practice in Regulations and Guidance*, HMSO, London.

Department of Health (DoH) (1991), *The Children Act, 1989: Guidance and Regulations*, vols. 1 and 2, HMSO, London.

Department of Health (DoH) (1995a), *Child Protection: Messages from Research*, HMSO, London.

Department of Health (DoH) (1995b), *The Challenge of Partnership in Child Protection: A Guide for Practitioners*, HMSO, London.

Department of Health (DoH) (1995c), *Looking After Children*, HMSO, London.

Department of Health (DoH) (1995d), *Social Work Decisions in Child Care: Recent Research Findings and their Implications*, HMSO, London.

Department of Health and Social Security (DHSS) (1985a), *Social Work Decisions in Child Care*, HMSO, London.

Department of Health and Social Security (DHSS) (1985b), *Review of Child Care Law: Report to Ministers of an Inter-Departmental Working Party*, HMSO, London.

Department of Social Welfare (1992), *Review of the Children Young Persons and Their Families Act 1989: Report of the Ministerial Review Team to the Minister of Social Welfare* (known as the *Mason Report*), Department of Social Welfare, Wellington.

Diorio, W.D. (1992), 'Parental Perceptions of the Authority of Public Child Welfare Caseworkers: Families in Society', *The Journal of Contemporary Human Services*, vol. 4, no. 3, pp. 55-64.

Dominelli, L. (1986), 'Power of the Powerless: Prostitution and the Reinforcement of Submissive Femininity', *Sociological Review*, vol. 34, no. 1, pp. 65-92.

Dominelli, L. (1988), *Anti-Racist Social Work*, BASW-Macmillan, London. Second edition published in 1997.

Dominelli, L. (1991), *Women Across Continents: Feminist Comparative Social Policy*, Harvester/Wheatsheaf, London.

Dominelli, L. (1997), *Sociology for Social Work*, Macmillan, London.

Dominelli, L. and Hoogvelt, A. (1996), 'Globalisation and the Technocratisation of Social Work', *Critical Social Policy*, no. 16, vol. 2, May, pp. 45-62.

Dominelli, L. and Gollins, T. (1997), 'Men, Power and Caring Relationships' *Sociological Review*, vol. 45, no. 3, August, pp. 396-415.

Dominelli, L. and McLeod, E. (1989), *Feminist Social Work*, Macmillan, London.

Eckelaar, J. (1992), 'The Importance of Thinking that Children have Rights', in P. Alston, S. Parker, and J. Seymour (eds), *Children, Rights and the Law*, Clarendon Press, Oxford.

Eichler, M. (1983), *Families in Canada Today*, Gage, Toronto.

Farmer, E. and Owen, M. (1995), *Child Protection Practice: Private Risks and Public Remedies - Decision-making, Intervention and Outcome in Child Protection Work*, HMSO, London.

Fisher, M., Marsh, P. and Phillips, D. (1986), *In and Out of Care: The Experiences of Children, Their Parents and Social Workers*, Batsford\BAAF, London.

Fox Harding, L. (1997), *Perspectives in Child Care Policy*, Second Edition, First published in 1991, Longman, London.

Franklin, B. (ed) (1986), *The Rights of Children*, Blackwell, Oxford.

Freeman, M.D.A. (1992a), *Children, their Families and the Law: Working with the Children Act*, Macmillan, London.

Freeman, M.D.A. (1992b), 'Taking Children's Rights more Seriously', *International Journal of Law and the Family*, vol. 6, pp. 52-71.

Freire, P. (1970), *Pedagogy of the Oppressed*, Seabury Press, New York.

Geddis, D.C. (1979), *Child Abuse: Report of a National Symposium held in Dunedin*, September, National Children's Health Research Foundation, Dunedin.

Gibbons, J., Conroy, S. and Ball, C. (1995), *Operating the Child Protection System*, HMSO, London.

Gordon, L. (1985), 'Child Abuse, Gender and the Myth of Family Independence: A Historical Critique', *Child Welfare*, vol. 64, no. 3, pp. 213-34.

Gordon, L. (1986), 'Feminism and Social Control: The Case of Child Abuse and Neglect' in J. Mitchell. and A. Oakley (eds), *What is Feminism? a Re-examination*, Pantheon Press, New York.

Gove, T.J. (1995), *The Report of the Gove Inquiry into Child Protection in British Columbia*, Province of British Columbia, Victoria.

Haig-Brown, C. (1988), *Resistance and Renewal: Surviving the Indian Residential School*, Tillicum Library/Arsenal Pulp Press, Vancouver.

Hamill, H. (1996), *Family Group Conferences in Child Care Practice*, University of East Anglia Monographs, Norwich.

Hassall, I. (1996), 'Origins and Development of Family Group Conferences', in J. Hudson, A. Morris, G. Maxwell and B. Galaway (eds), *Family Group Conferences: Perspectives on Policy and Practice*, The Federation Press, Annandale, NSW.

Hassall, I. and Maxwell, G. (1991), *The Family Group Conference: A Report from the Office of the Commissioner for Children*, Department of Social Welfare, Wellington.

Hetherington, R. (1998), 'Issues in European Child Protection Research', *European Journal of Social Work*, vol. 1, no. 1, pp. 71-82.

Hill, M. and Aldgate, J. (1996), *Child Welfare Services: Developments in Law, Policy, Practice and Research*, Jessica Kingsley, London.

Holman, B. (1992), 'Flaws in Partnership', *Community Care*, 20 February, pp. 12-16.

Holman, R. (1988), *Putting Families First*, Macmillan, London.

Home Office (1997), *Tackling Youth Crime: A Consultation Paper*, Home Office, London.

Home Office, Department of Health, Department of Education and Science, and Welsh Office (1991), *Working Together under the Children Act 1989: A Guide to Arrangements for Interagency Working for the Protection of Children from Abuse*, HMSO, London.

Hudson, J., Morris, A., Maxwell, G. and Galaway, B. (1996), *Family Group Conferences: Perspectives on Policy and Practice*. The Federation Press - Criminal Justice Press, London.

Hutchison, E. (1992), 'Child Welfare as a Woman's Issue: Families in Society', in *The Journal of Contemporary Human Services*, February, pp. 67-77.

Illich, I. (1972), *Deschooling Society*, Harper and Row Publishers, New York.

Jackson, S. E. (1998), 'Family Group Conferencing in Youth Justice: Issues for Implementation in England and Wales', *The Howard Journal of Criminal Justice*, vol. 37, no.1, pp. 34-51.

Kahn, S. (1982), *Organising*, McGraw-Hill Book Company, New York.

Kelleher, P. and Whelan, M. (1992), *Dublin Communities in Action*, Combat Poverty Agency, Dublin, Canada.

Kirkwood, A. (1992), *The Leicestershire Inquiry 1992*, Leicestershire County Council, Leicester.

Krane, J. (1994), *The Transformation of Women into Mother Protectors: An Examination of Child Protection Practices in Cases of Child Sexual Abuse*. Unpublished doctoral dissertation, University of Toronto, School of Social Work.

Kretzman, J. and McKnight, J. (1993), *Building Communities from the Inside Out*, Centre for Urban Affairs and Policy Research, Evanston, Illinois.

Kymlicka, W. (1992), *Recent Work in Citizenship Theory*, Corporate Policy and Research, Multiculturalism and Citizenship Canada, Ottawa.

Lakey, B., Lakey, G., Napier, R. and Robinson, J. (1995), *Grassroots and Non-Profit Leadership*, New Society Publishers, Philadelphia, PA.

Lakey, G. (1987), *Powerful Peace Making*, New Society Press, Philadelphia,. PA.

Lansdown, G. (1995) 'Children's Rights and Wrongs', *Poverty*, vol. 90, no. 2.

Lee, B. (1992), *Pragmatics of Community Organisation*, Second edition, Commonact Press, Mississauga.

Lee, B., McGrath, G., Moffatt, S. and Usha, K.G. (1996), 'Community Practice Education in Canadian Schools of Social Work', *Canadian Social Work Review*, vol. 13, no. 2, pp. 221-236.

Levy, A. and Kahan, B. (1991), *The Pindown Experience and the Protection of Children*, Staffordshire County Council, Stafford.

L'Huiller, E. (1994), *Neglecting Mothers: A Feminist Analysis of the Victorian Child Protection System*, Unpublished Masters thesis, University of Melbourne, Women's Studies, Department of History, Melbourne.

Lilja, J. (1997), *The Family Group Conference Project in Sweden*, Unpublished paper presented at the International Forum on FGCs, Winchester, 2-4 June, 1997.

Little, M. (1993), 'Specialist Residential Services for Difficult Adolescents: Some Recent Research Findings', in R. Bullock (ed), *Problem Adolescents*, Whiting and Birch, London.

Lupton, C., Barnard, S. and Swall-Yarrington, S. (1995), *Family Planning? An Evaluation of the Family Group Conference Model*, Social Services Research and Information Unit (SSRIU), Portsmouth University.

Lupton, C. and Stevens, M. (1997), *Family Outcomes: Following through on Family Group Conferences*, Report No. 34, SSRIU, University of Portsmouth.

MacIntyre, E. (1993), 'The Historical Context of Child Welfare in Canada', in B. Wharf (ed), *Rethinking Child Welfare in Canada*, McClelland and Stewart Inc., Toronto.

MacLeod, L. (1980), *Wife Battering in Canada: The Vicious Circle*, Canadian Advisory Council on the Status of Women, Ottawa.

Magura, S. and Moses, B. (1984), 'Clients as Evaluators in Child Protective Services', in *Child Welfare*, LXIII, no. 2, March-April, pp. 99-112.

Mason, J. (1993), *Child Welfare Policy: Critical Australian Perspectives*, Hale and Ironmonger, Sydney.

Maxwell, G.M. and Morris, A. (1992), 'The Family Group Conference: A New Paradigm for Making Decisions about Children and Young People', *Children Australia*, vol. 17, pp. 11-15.

Maxwell, G.M. and Morris, A. (1993), *Families, Victims and Culture: Youth Justice in New Zealand*, Social Policy Agency and Institute of Criminology, Wellington.

Mayo, M. (1977), 'Community Development or Social Change' in R. Bailey and

M. Brake (eds), *Radical Social Work,* Edward Arnold, London, pp. 129-143.

McElrea, F.W.M. (1995), *Accountability in the Community: Taking Responsibility for Offending,* A paper prepared for the Legal Research Foundation Conference, Auckland.

McKay, R.A. (1981), *Children in Foster Care - An Examination of the Case Histories of a Sample of Children in Care with Particular Emphasis on Placement of Children in Foster Homes,* Department of Social Welfare, Wellington.

McKnight, J. (1996), *The Careless Society: Community and its Counterfeits.* Basic Books, New York.

McQuaig, L. (1995), *Shooting the Hippo,* Penguin Books, Toronto.

Millham, S., Bullock, R., Hosie, K. and Little, M. (1986), *Lost in Care: The Problem of Maintaining Links between Children in Care and their Families,* Gower, Aldershot.

Millham, S., Bullock, R., Hosie, K. and Little, M. (1989), *Access Disputes in Child Care,* Gower, Aldershot.

Ministerial Advisory Committee (1986), *Puao-Te-Ata-Tu: The Report of the Ministerial Advisory Committee on a Maori Perspective for the Department of Social Welfare,* Department of Social Welfare, Wellington.

Mishra, R. (1990), *The Welfare State in Capitalist Society,* University of Toronto Press, Toronto.

Mittler, H. (1992), 'Crossing Frontiers', *Community Care,* 12 November 1992, pp. 22-3.

Moore, D. (1995), *A New Approach to Juvenile Justice: An Evaluation of Family Group Conferencing in Wagga Wagga,* Centre for Rural Social Research, Wagga Wagga, NSW.

Moreau, M. and Leonard, L. (1989), *Empowerment through a Structural Approach to Social Work,* Carleton University, School of Social Work, Ottawa.

Morris, K. (1994), 'Family Group Conferences in the UK' , in J. Tunnard (ed), *Family Group Conferences: A Report Commissioned by the Department of Health,* Family Rights Group, London.

Morris, K. (1995), *Family Group Conference: An Introductory Pack,* Family Rights Group, London.

Morris, K., Marsh, P. and Wiffen, J. (1998) *A Training Pack for Family Group Conferences,* Family Rights Group, London.

Morris, K. and Tunnard, J. (1996), *Family Group Conferences: Messages from UK Practice and Research,* Family Rights Group, London.

Mowbray, M. (1985), 'The Medicinal Properties of Localism', in R. Thorpe and J. Petrochina (eds), *Community Work or Social Change?,* Routledge and Kegan Paul, London.

Moyer, B. (1990), *The Practical Strategist,* Social Movement Empowerment Project, San Francisco.

Mullender, A. (1996), *Rethinking Domestic Violence: The Social Work and Probation Responses*, Routledge, London.

Mullender, A. and Ward, D. (1991), *Self-Directed Groupwork: Users take Action for Empowerment*, Whiting and Birch, London.

Murphy, C.G. (1954), *Community Organisation Practice*, Houghton, Mifflin Company, Boston.

National Children's and Youth Law Centre (1995), *Rights Now!*, vol. 3, no. 4, University of New South Wales, Sydney, Australia, pp. 1-3.

National Council of Welfare (1977), *Another Look at Welfare Reform*, Minister of Public Works and Government Services Canada, Ottawa.

Nava, M. (1988), 'Cleveland and the Press: Outrage and Anxiety in the Reporting of Child Sexual Abuse', *Feminist Review*, no. 28, Spring, pp. 103-121.

Newbury, D. (1989), *Stop Spadina: Citizens Against an Expressway*, Commonact Press, Toronto.

Nixon, P. (1992), *Family Group Conferences: A Radical Approach to Planning the Care and Protection of Children*, Unpublished paper, Hampshire County Council, Winchester.

Novick, M. and Volpe, R. (1989), 'Perspectives on Social Practice', *Children at Risk Project*, the Laidlaw Foundation, Toronto.

Office for National Statistics (1997), *Social Focus on Families*, HMSO, London.

O'Hagan, K. (ed) (1996), *Competence in Social Work: A Practical Guide for Professionals*, Jessica Kingsley, London.

Oswin, H. (1984), *Community Development Work in Child Welfare*, Unpublished Master's Research Project, McMaster University, Hamilton.

Packman, J. (1993), 'From Prevention to Partnership: Child Welfare Services across Three Decades', in G. Pugh (ed), *Thirty Years of Change for Children*, National Children's Bureau, London.

Packman, J., Randall, J. and Jacques, N. (1986), *Who Needs Care? Social Work Decisions about Children*, Blackwell, London.

Parton, C. and Parton, N. (1989), 'Women, the Family and Child Protection', *Critical Social Policy*, pp. 39-49.

Parton, N. (1991), *Governing the Family: Child Care, Child Protection and the State*, Macmillan, London.

Paterson, K. and Harvey, M. (1991), *Organisation and Operation of Care and Protection: Family Group Conferences*, Evaluation Unit, Department of Social Welfare, Wellington.

Pelton, L. (1978), 'Child Abuse and Neglect: The Myth of Classlessness', *American Journal of Orthopsychiatry*, 48, pp. 4.

Pendergrast, M. (1993), *First of All, Do No Harm*, Skeptic, Denver.

Pennell, J. and Burford, G. (1994), 'Widening the Circle: Family Group Decision-making', *Journal of Child and Youth Care*, vol. 9, pp. 1-11.

Pennell, J. and Burford, G. (1997), 'Addressing Domestic Violence through Family Group Decision-making', Unpublished paper presented at the International Forum on Family Group Conferences, 2-4 June, Winchester.

Pilalis J., Tanielu, Rev. M. and Opai, S. (1988), *Dangerous Situations*, Department of Social Welfare, Wellington.

Pinker, R. (1971), *Social Theory and Social Policy*, Heinemann Educational Books Ltd., London.

Piven, F.F. and Cloward, R.A. (1977), *Poor People's Movements*, Pantheon Books, New York.

Plant, R. (1974), *Community and Ideology,* Routledge and Kegan Paul, London.

Preston-Shoot, M. (1992), 'Empowerment, Partnership and Authority in Groupwork Practice: A Training Contribution', *Groupwork*, vol. 5, no. 2, pp. 5-30.

Prevention Team (1997) , *Prevention Team Framework*, Children's Aid Society of Metropolitan Toronto, Toronto.

Pringle, K. (1992/3), 'Child Sexual Abuse Perpetrated by Welfare Personnel and the Problem of Men', *Critical Social Policy*, vol. 12, no. 3, pp. 4-19.

Renouf, J., Robb, G. and Walls. P. (1990), *Children, Young Persons and their Families Act 1989: Report of the First Year of Operation,* Department of Social Welfare, Wellington.

Repo, M. (1977), 'The Fallacy of Community Control', in J. Cowley, A. Kaye, M. Mayo and M. Thompson (eds), *Community or Class Struggle,* Stage 1, London, pp. 47-64.

Rice, J. (1990), 'Volunteering to Build a Stronger Community', *Perceptions*, vol. 14, no. 4, Autumn, pp. 9-16.

Rifkin, J. (1995), *The End of Work*, G. P. Putnam's Sons, New York.

Ross, M.G. (1972), *Community Organisation*, Second edition, Harper and Row Publishers, New York.

Rothman, J. and Tropman, J.E. (1987), 'Models of Community Organisation and Macro-Practice Perspectives: Their Mixing and Phasing', in F.M. Cox, J.L. Erlich, J. Rothman and J.E. Tropman (eds), *Strategies of Community Organisation*, Peacock Press, Ithaca, pp. 3-26.

Rowe, J., Cain, H., Hundleby, M. and Keane, A. (1984), *Long Term Foster Care,* Batsford/BAAF, London.

Rowe, J., Hundleby, M. and Garnett, L. (1989), *Child Care Now: A Survey of Child Care Patterns,* BAAF Research Series 6, London.

Rubin, R.J. and Rubin, I. (1986), *Community Organisation and Development*, Merrill Publishing Company, Toronto.

Russel-Erlich, J. and Rivera, F.G. (1986), 'Community Empowerment as a Non-Problem', *Journal of Sociology and Social Welfare*, September, no. 3, pp.451-465.

Ryan, M. (1993), *The Children Act 1989: Putting it into Practice*, Arena, Aldershot.

Ryburn, M. (1992), 'Family Group Conferences', in J. Thoburn (ed), *Practice in Participation: Involving Families in Child Protection*, HMSO, London.

Ryburn, M. (1994a), 'Planning for Children Here and in New Zealand: A Comparison of the Legislation', in J. Tunnard (ed), *Family Group Conferences: A Report Commissioned by the Department of Health*, Family Rights Group, London.

Ryburn, M. (1994b), 'Contact after Contested Adoptions', *Adoption and Fostering*, vol. 18, pp. 30-8.

Ryburn, M. and Atherton, C. (1996), 'Family Group Conferences: Partnership in Practice', *Adoption and Fostering*, vol. 20, pp. 16-23.

Saul, J.R. (1997), *The Uunconscious Civilisation*, Anansi, Toronto.

Scarth, S., Wharf, B. and Tyrwhitt, E. (eds) (1995), *A Special Issue of Child Welfare*, vol. LXXIV, no. 3, May/June, pp. 486-502.

Scarth, S., Wharf, B., and Tyrwhitt, E. (eds) (1995b), *Changing the Child Welfare Agenda: Contributions from Canada*, University of Toronto Press, Toronto.

Schmidt, B. D. (1978), *Child Protection Team Handbook*, STPM Press, New York.

Shapland, J., Willmore, J. and Duff, P. (1985), *Victims in the Criminal Justice System*, Gower, Aldershot.

Sinclair, R., Garnett, L. and Berridge, D. (1995), *Social Work and Assessment with Adolescents*, National Children's Bureau, London.

Smith, B. and Smith, T. (1990), 'For Love and Money: Women as Foster Mothers', *Affilia*, vol. 5, no. 1, pp. 66-80.

Standing Committee on Health and Welfare, Social Affairs, Seniors and the Status of Women (1993), *Towards 2000: Eliminating Child Poverty*, Queen's Printer, Ottawa.

Stedman Jones, G. (1971), *Outcast London*, Clarendon Press, Oxford.

Swift, K.J. (1991), 'Contradictions in Child Welfare: Neglect and Responsibility', in C. Baines, P. Evans and S. Neysmith (eds), *Women's Caring: Feminist Perspectives on Social Welfare*, McClelland and Stewart Inc., Toronto.

Swift, K. J., (1995), 'Manufacturing 'Bad Mothers': A Critical Perspective on Child Neglect', in S. Scarth, B. Wharf and E. Tyrwhitt, *Changing the Child Welfare Agenda: Contributions from Canada*, University of Toronto Press, Toronto.

Tapp, P.F. (1990), 'Family Group Conferences and the Children, Young Persons and their Families Act 1989: An Ineffective Statute?', *New Zealand Recent Law Review*, pp. 82-88.

Thoburn, J., Lewis, A. and Shemmings, D. (1995), *Paternalism or Partnership? Family Involvement in the Child Protection Process*, HMSO, London.

Thoburn, J. and Rowe, J. (1988) 'Research: A Snapshot of Permanent Family Placement', *Adoption and Fostering*, vol. 2, no. 3, pp. 52-71.

Thomas, D.N. (1983),'Participation in Politics and the Community', in D.N. Thomas (ed), *The Making of Community Work,* George Allen and Unwin Ltd, London.

Thornton, C. (1993), *Family Group Conferences: A Literature Review,* Practitioners Publishing, Lower Hutt.

Thorpe, R. (1993), 'Empowerment Groupwork with Parents of Children in Care', in J. Mason (ed), *Child Welfare Policy: Critical Australian Perspectives,* Hale and Ironmonger, Sydney.

United Nations Development Programme (UNDP) (1998), *Human Development Report,* United Nations, New York.

Utting, W. (1991), *Children in the Public Care System,* HMSO, London.

Von Dadelzen, J. (1987), *Sexual Abuse Study, An Examination of the Histories of Sexual Abuse among Girls Currently in the Care of the Department of Social Welfare,* Department of Social Welfare, Wellington.

Walgrave, L. (1995), 'Restorative Justice for Juveniles: Just a Technique or a Fully Fledged Alternative?,' *The Howard Journal,* vol. 34, pp. 228-249.

Warren, R. (1983),'Observations on the State of Community Theory', in R. Warren and L. Lyons (eds), *New Perspectives on the American Community,* Dorey Press, Homewood Ill.

Wedge, P. and Mantle, G. (1991), *Sibling Groups and Social Work: A Study of Children Released for Permanent Family Placement,* Avebury, Aldershot.

Wharf, B. (1979), 'Theory and Practice', in B. Wharf (ed), *Community Work in Canada,* McClelland and Stewart Inc., Toronto, pp. 9-24.

Wharf, B. (1997), 'Community Organisation: Canadian Experiences', in B. Wharf and M. Clague, (eds), *Community Organising: Canadian Experiences,* University of Toronto Press, Toronto, pp. 1-14.

Wharf, B. (ed) (1993), *Rethinking Child Welfare in Canada,* McClelland and Stewart Inc., Toronto.

White, R. and Lowe, N. (1991), *The Children Act, 1989: Working in Partnership with Families - A Reader,* vol. 1, HMSO, London.

Wilcox, R., Smith, D., Moore, J., Hewitt, A., Allan, G., Walker, H., Ropatu, M., Monu, L. and Featherstone, T. (1991), *Family Decision-making: Family Group Conferences, Practitioners Views,* Practitioners Publishing, Lower Hutt.

Wilkinson, R.G. (1994), *Unfair Shares: The Effects of Widening Income Differences on the Welfare of Young Children,* Barnardo's, Iford.

Williams, M. (1997), *Parents, Children and Social Workers: Working in Partnership under the Children Act, 1989,* Avebury, Aldershot.

Wolkind, S. (1979), *Medical Aspects of Adoption and Foster Care,* Heinneman Medical Books, London.

Wright, M. (1991), *Justice for Victims and Offenders,* Open University Press, Milton Keynes.

Wright, M. (1995), 'Victims, Mediation and Criminal Justice', *Criminal Law Review*, pp. 187-99.

Index

209